Alastair Sawday's

# Special
## places to stay

PORTUGAL

Edited by John Dalton

| | |
|---|---|
| Typesetting, Conversion & Repro: ..... | Avonset, Bath |
| Maps: .......... | Bartholomew Mapping Services, a division of HarperCollins Publishers, Glasgow |
| Printing: .......... | Stige, Italy |
| Design: .......... | Caroline King & Springboard Design, Bristol |
| UK Distribution: .......... | Portfolio, Greenford, Middlesex |
| US Distribution: .......... | The Globe Pequot Press, Guilford, Connecticut |

Published in March 2001

Alastair Sawday Publishing Co. Ltd
The Home Farm Stables, Barrow Gurney, Bristol BS48 3RW

The Globe Pequot Press
P. O. Box 480
Guilford, Connecticut 06437
USA

First edition.



A catalogue record for this book is available from the British Library.



ISBN 1-901970-17-5 in the UK

ISBN 0-7627-0888-3 in the US

Printed in Italy

Alastair Sawday's

# Special

## places to stay

## Portugal

"How often did I bless the hour when my steps
were directed to Portugal!"
*William Beckford*

The
Globe
Pequot
Press

Guilford
Connecticut, USA

ASP

Alastair Sawday Publishing
Bristol, UK

# Contents

# Acknowledgements

John Dalton loves music, good company and writing. He also loves all those things that make you want to visit Portugal again and again: its gracious, proud, friendly people, the sights, sounds and smells of a country that has everything from sun-drenched beaches to rolling vineyard terraces, not forgetting the fabulous food, fine wines and fado.

Like many of us, he loves paperwork and computers less but with good humour and plenty of calming harp chords, he rose to the challenges that compiling a book like this brings and survives to tell the tale. He deserves much praise for pulling it off.

So, too, does Carol Dymond who has searched out a whole range of special places. Her own home is included here and those who meet her will find a warm-hearted, independent woman with strong environmental values that she strives to live by. We salute her. Robert and Mary Stephens did sterling work too, with great efficiency and attention to detail.

On the office front, Emma Carey has steadfastly pursued and pinned down the final details with unassuming determination and Julia Richardson has worked with volumes of energy and good grace to bring the project to production. Thanks too to the rest of the ASP office team; also to Marie Hodges for lending us her Portuguese, and to David Griffiths, Roger Parsons, Jayne Warren... This is beginning to sound like the 'Oscars' ...

*AS*

| | |
|---|---|
| Series Editor: | Alastair Sawday |
| Editor: | John Dalton |
| Managing Editor: | Annie Shillito |
| Production Manager: | Julia Richardson |
| Administration: | Emma Carey, Kate Harris |
| Accounts: | Jenny Purdy |
| Additional inspections: | Carol Dymond<br>Robert & Mary Stephens |

*Muito obrigado* (special thanks) to Mini Pimental Scarlett, José and Isabel Alberty and Sangeeta and Kai.

# Introduction

This is our first book to be devoted entirely to Portugal - not a moment too soon. Hitherto it has been part of the 'Spain and Portugal' book of Special Places but we have yielded to a growing clamour for a separate book.

John Dalton, who once lived there, has weaved his way from top to bottom of this small but richly endowed country, unearthing the beautiful, the serene, the interesting and the architecturally blessed. But that is only half of it; he has found some lovely people, the sort one wants to spend time with, whose houses provide relief from the rigours of modern travel.

A strong feature of all our books is the people in them, some of whom have thrown off the shackles of modern urban life in exchange for rural serenity. They have, of course, found other things along the way: blisters and bruises, rumpled dignity, difficult builders, inflated bills, crumbling walls, dry wells, shallow foundations and reluctant planners. However, all the people whose stories are writ large in the book have drawn on deep reserves of determination and have triumphed. The results are simply wonderful.

If you are well-connected you will be able to travel around Portugal staying in fine old houses with interesting people whose families draw on roots put down centuries ago. If not, you can have your fun with this book, for it is an open-sesame to houses and people. You won't have to drive past peering hopelessly through imposing gates, or gaze at a set of ochre-crumbling walls and wish you could be behind them. You won't have to listen impotently to stories in the village bar of 'those fascinating people' up the road; you can go and stay with them. Above all, you won't - like many guests - feel that you should move on after two nights because you have outstayed your welcome.

So, with this wonderful book in your hand your free-wheeling holiday in Portugal will be exhilarating and rewarding. You will find an unusually eclectic gathering of places, so read carefully above and between the lines to discover which places would best suit you. And please tell us about your own discoveries.

*Alastair Sawday*

# Introduction

## How do we choose our Special Places?

In identifying a 'special' place the single most important factor is probably *personality*, which is generally what makes our favourite people special to us, too. When we think of houses we may be attracted primarily to the location, architecture, contents, history, views, but the most significant factor in terms of staying there will be the personality of the hosts.

The beautiful is that which reveals its true nature; real ugliness stems from falsity. As with people, so with houses. Beauty can be experienced in a cottage, built long ago according to tradition, and in materials which belong to the landscape, and in a consciously created manor house, castle or palace; the difference may be compared with that between a folk tune which has endured centuries or an orchestral work created by a great composer consciously in touch with the folk roots (music contains architecture and vice versa). Then there are those properties (and melodies) which are more a product of their time than of place.

In any of these places we may discover something special. It may stem from the personality of the current owners that pervades the house, or it may have been built into the fabric of the place long ago by the founders or architect. This means that a small modern *pensão* can be as special in its way as a hotel, or a castle or monastery. Whatever sort of place it is, it will be run by good people, whether by a family who will welcome you to the dinner table as an old friend (the Portuguese are very hospitable) or staff who are discreet and helpful in a place where you are smitten by the architectural wonders, and exquisite furniture and antiques.

There has probably never been a better time to stay in Portugal, particularly since the advent of *Turismo de habitação* and *Turismo rural*, which has encouraged owners of historic and rural homes to open their doors to guests. Portugal is not a large country, but it has a wonderfully long history and great variations in landscape and character, and the old houses particularly are among the finest in the world: it is surprising how often, for example, we have discovered houses where the same family has lived for several centuries; what a treat it is to enjoy a small slice of that tradition. Then there are the more modern homes, full of light and space, and now the growing number of places which combine holidays with a focus on alternative spiritual and physical practices; this, I think will be a growing trend in holidays in Portugal, a country which offers a rich culture, a benign climate and very good food.

# Introduction

There is the other side of Portugal, too, of course, epitomised by the uncontrolled development of incongruous buildings, domestic and touristic. You can hardly travel anywhere (in the world) without seeing examples of that, but we avert our gaze and eschew the ugly, the dreary and the mass-produced look of chain hotels. We also ignore unfriendly hotels, noisy ones, or those which are over-priced.

## What to expect

In most cases you will be staying in someone's home - people who have families, jobs, sometimes pets, and friends. We choose them because we know they'll do a good job of looking after you. The Portuguese are very convivial people who love the good things in life: company, conversation and good food and drink, so be prepared to be swept along by it all.

## Finding the right place for you

It's our job to help you find a place you will like. We give honest descriptions of our houses and owners and you should glean from the write-up what the owners or housekeeper or staff are like and how formal or casual the place is. The mention of beautiful antiques should alert you to the fact that this may not be the place to take your toddler, and phrases such as 'dress for dinner' tell you that this isn't a place to slop around in shorts and t-shirt. You should also be able to tell if it's the sort of place where you can become a temporary member of the family or, somewhere where you can have as much privacy as you like.

In each write-up there are clues about the mood of the house, and there is an enormous variety within this book. The older or larger ones may seem more immediately appealing, but don't overlook the modern ones - they often have great personality, too. In any place, it's always the owners or staff who have the biggest influence on the atmosphere you experience.

## How to use this book

### Map

Look at the map at the front of the book, find your area then look for the places which are mapped. Note their numbers and look up the same entry number which you will find at the bottom of the page, in colour. The actual page number is different. If you prefer to browse through the book and let the individual entries make up your mind, then simply check the map reference at the bottom of the page.

# Introduction

### Rooms

We tell you the range of accommodation in single, double, twin or triple rooms or in apartments, suites, cottages or houses. Extra beds can often be added for children. Check when booking.

### Bathrooms

'With bath & wc' in our entries means the bathroom is directly off the bedroom.

Those of you who like your bath should know that the length of baths can vary from half to full length. In the south where water is such a precious commodity you may prefer to shower. And when you are packing do put in a bar of soap; the more simple hostal type-places occasionally don't give you any and many of the hotels will only have those minute throw-away soaps which are so difficult to find when you drop them in the bath.

In hotels, don't pull the cord which dangles above your bath unless you are in dire straits. It is an alarm and may bring your friendly receptionist rushing to your side.

### Prices

These are mostly given in Escudos - a few are in Sterling and Euros - and room prices are, in the case of doubles and twins, for the room for two people per night. Prices for meals, however, are per person.

The prices we quote were applicable at the time that this book went to press. We publish every two years so expect prices to be higher if you are using this book in 2002 or early 2003.

### Symbols

There is an explanation of these on the last page of the book. Use them as a guide, not an unequivocal fact. If an owner has a 'pets welcome' symbol, check in advance that your pet will be welcome. Some told us that they only accept 'small' pets, so will that include your Irish wolfhound puppies? Find out. Equally, if an owner does not have the symbol that you're looking for, it's worth discussing your needs; the Portuguese generally love to please.

### Phones & Phone Codes

From Portugal to another country: dial 00 then add the country code and then the area code without the first 0. Eg ASP in Bristol, from Portugal: UK No. 01275 464891 becomes 00 44 1275 464891

# Introduction

Within Portugal: simply dial the numbers given.

Calling Portugal from another country:
From the USA: 011 351 then the number
From the UK: 00 351 then the number

Land line numbers begin with 2, mobile phone numbers with 9 (and are more expensive).

The Portuguese phone system works well, and as well as public phone boxes (for which you can buy phonecards in most newsagents) and phone boxes inside post offices (look for *Correios*), virtually every café has a phone for which customers pay the *impulsos* used, counted on a meter. (Café phones cost more.)

## Types of Properties

These pages reveal a plethora of different terms to describe the various hostelries. We include no star ratings in our guides; we feel they are limiting and often misleading. We prefer to guide with our description of any particular place. This list serves as a rough guide to what you might expect to find behind each name.

| | |
|---|---|
| *Albergaria* | An upmarket inn. |
| *Casa* | A house; it may be old or new. |
| *Castelo* | A castle. |
| *Estalagem* | An inn; more expensive than an *albergaria*. |
| *Heredade* | A large farm or estate. |
| *Paço* | A palace or country house. |
| *Palacio* | A palace or country house. Grander than a *paço*.. |
| *Pensão* | A guesthouse; the Portuguese equivalent of a bed and breakfast, though breakfast is not always included. |
| *Quinta* | A country estate or villa; in the Douro wine-growing area it often refers to a wine lodge's property. |
| *Residencial* | A guesthouse; usually slightly more expensive than a *pensao* and normally serving breakfast. |
| *Solar* | Manor house. |

# Introduction

## Practical Matters

*Meals*

We tell you if the owners offer lunches and dinners, and give an average price (and note that these are per person, unlike room prices). In many it is necessary to give advance notice. It's often more relaxing to eat in say, after a long journey, than go out again, but Portugal has so many restaurants and cafés that whether you're in town, village or country, there will be a place offering freshly-cooked food nearby.

It is surprisingly inexpensive to eat out in Portugal. The set meal - *ementa turistica* - may offer a small choice while à la carte - *á lista* - is a full choice. The dish of the day - *prato do día* - is usually a local speciality and helpings can be enormous. It is perfectly normal to ask for a *meia dose* - half portion - or for two adults to ask for *uma dose* - a portion - to share between two.

When you sit down at virtually any restaurant in Portugal you will be given things to nibble before your meal arrives - olives, *chouriço* (spicy sausage), sardine spread. Do remember - you will be charged for whatever you eat.

*Bacalão* - salt cod - is the national dish: there are said to be 365 different ways of preparing it! Pork (as in Spain) is also much used. And don't despise the humble sardine - it is often the cheapest item on the menu and can be very good. The basic mix for the ubiquitous *salada mista* is tomatoes, onions and olives. You can ask for it *sem ólio* - without oil. Puddings are normally very sweet.

## Seasons and Public Holidays

In Portugal everything closes down at Easter and Christmas and on the following public holidays:

| | |
|---|---|
| **April 25** | Commemorating the 1974 Revolution |
| **May 1** | Labour Day. |
| **Corpus Christi** | - usually early June. |
| **June 10** - | Dia de camões e das Comunidades - Camões day. |
| **August 15** - | the Feast of the Assumption. |
| **October 5** - | Republic Day. |
| **November 1** - | All Saints Day. |
| **December 1** - | Immaculate Conception. |

# Introduction

There are also festivals for the saints and other commemorations. The
Portuguese love festivals and there are lots during the summer. If there's
one on near you, don't miss it. Here are some of the major festivals:

## May

*Queima das Fitas* - celebrating the end of the academic year in Coimbra.
*Fátima* -Portugal's most famous pilgrimage; also in October.

## June

*Feira Nacional* at Santarém lasts for 10 days, starting on the first Friday.
*Festa de São Gonçalo* in Amarente; first weekend.
*Santos Popularos* in Lisbon - celebrations in honour of St Anthony (13th),
St John (24th) and St Peter (29th). There is also a festival in Porto for St
John on the same date.

## July

*Festa do Colete Encarnado* in Vila Franca de Xira with Pamplona-style
running of bulls through the streets; first two weeks.

## August

*Romaria da Nossa Senhora da Agonía* in Viana do Castelo; third weekend.

## September

*Romaria da Nossa Senhora dos Remédios* in Lamego. Pilgrimage from
6th-8th.
*'New Fair'* in Ponte de Lima; second and third weekend.

## October

*Feira de Outubro* in Vila France de Xira - more bull running.
*Fátima* - second great pilgrimage of the year.

## November

*Feira Nacional do Cavalo* - National Horse Fair in Golegã.

*Booking*

Try to book well ahead if you plan to be in Portugal during holidays.
August is very busy in the tourist and beach areas so you might choose,
then, to head for the more remote places in this book. Many hotels will
ask you for a credit card number when you make your reservation. And
remember to let smaller places know if you want dinner.

There's a bilingual booking form at the back of the book. Hotels often
send back a signed or stamped copy as confirmation. E-mail culture is still
in its early days in Portugal. Hotels don't necessarily assume that you are
expecting a speedy reply!

# Introduction

## Cancellations

Please give as much notice as possible.

## Registration

Many city hotels will only hold a reservation until the early evening, even though you might have booked months in advance. So ring ahead to let them know if you are planning to arrive late. (It remains law that you should register on arrival in a hotel. Hotels have no right, once you have done so, to keep your passport.)

## Payment

Cash is always an acceptable method of payment but many places in this book also accept payment by credit card and have that symbol. The most commonly accepted credit cards are Visa, MasterCard and Eurocard. Many smaller places don't take plastic because of high bank charges; these will be marked with the 'piggy bank' symbol. There is nearly always a cash dispenser (ATM) close at hand; again Visa, MasterCard and Eurocard are the most useful.

## Euros

The Euro will be introduced into Portugal during the period of this guide's validity and at first will operate in parallel with the escudo. By 2002 it will be fully operational. We include a conversion chart at the end of this book.

## Plugs

Virtually all sockets now have 220/240 AC voltage (usually 2-pin). Pack an adaptor if you travel with electrical appliances.

## Driving & Car Hire

Driving in Portugal, especially the north, requires patience. The maps at the front of this book are to give you an approximate idea of where places are but do take a detailed road map with you. The worst time to drive is on any of the public holidays listed earlier when there is a massive exodus towards the country and the beach.

It is compulsory to have in the car: a spare set of bulbs, a warning triangle, a fire extinguisher and a basic first aid kit.

Don't forget your driving licence: if you are hiring a car you will need it and it is an offence to drive without it.

And remember that foreign number plates attract attention in the big cities so never leave your car with valuables inside. Use a public car park; they are cheap and safe.

# Introduction

## Public Transport

You meet more people, and get much more of a feel for the country by travelling this way. Portugal is not a large country and you can get almost everywhere easily and efficiently by train or bus. Trains are often cheaper and some lines are very scenic, but it's almost always quicker to go by bus - especially on shorter journeys. If you are planning a quick trip by bus avoid buses marked *carreiras* (or CR). *Carreiras* might mean 'in a hurry' but these are the slowest of slow local buses and stop everywhere.

## Security

A degree of caution is necessary in the larger cities especially in the narrow side streets. Best not to carry ostentatious bags or cameras.

## Children

The Portuguese love children, and most houses have the 'children welcome' symbol; indeed, most owners were surprised that we even asked the question. The absence of it means different things in different houses; some houses will welcome babies but don't relish the thought of youngsters tearing along corridors lined with antiques and figurines, so do enquire if the place appeals. We found that most owners have a flexible attitude.

## Pets

Some people can't bear to leave home without transporting a beast of some sort with them, and the 'Pets welcome' symbol means you can probably take your animal into the home; the criteria vary, often according to size and level of training (see Symbols above). Livestock may be allowed in bedrooms or housed outside. Do check in advance.

## Smoking

Many Portuguese like to smoke, and it's particularly noticeable in restaurants and cafés. Most houses have no restrictions, but a growing number are introducing some sort of segregation and offering smoke-free rooms.

## Tipping

In restaurants the 10% service charge is usually included in the bill; in places where your bill is brought by a waiter, you should add 10% or so.

## Portuguese Tourist Offices

UK - 2nd floor, 22/25a Sackville Street, London W1X 1DE.
Tel: 0207 494 1441

USA - 590 Fifth Avenue, New York 10022. Tel: 212 354 4403

# Introduction

### Environment

We seek to reduce our impact on the environment where possible by:

- Planting trees to compensate for our carbon emissions (as calculated by Edinburgh University); we are officially a 'carbon-neutral company'.
- Re-using paper, recycling stationery, tins, bottles, etc.
- Encouraging staff use of bicycles (they're given free) and car-sharing.
- Celebrating the use of organic, home and locally produced food.
- Publishing books that support, in however small a way, the rural economy and small-scale businesses.

### Subscriptions

Owners pay to appear in this guide; their fee goes towards the high production costs of an all-colour book. We only include places and owners that we find special. It is not possible for anyone to buy their way in.

### Special Places to Stay on the Internet

8000 people a month 'visit' the site, and we think you should join them! Not only do they have access to honest and up-to-date information about hundreds of places to stay across Europe, but they can buy any of our books via our window on the world wide web: www.sawdays.co.uk

### Disclaimer

We make no claims to pure objectivity in judging our special places to stay. They are here because we like them. Our opinions and tastes are ours alone and this book is a statement of them; we hope that you will share them.

We have done our utmost to get our facts right but apologise unreservedly for any mistakes that may have crept in. Sometimes, too, prices shift, usually upwards and 'things' change. We would be grateful to be told of any errors or changes, however small.

### And finally

A huge thank you to all those who have taken the time to share your opinions with us. They help us improve the Special Places to Stay series

Please continue to send us your comments; there is a report form at the back of this book. Or e-mail us at portugal@sawdays.co.uk

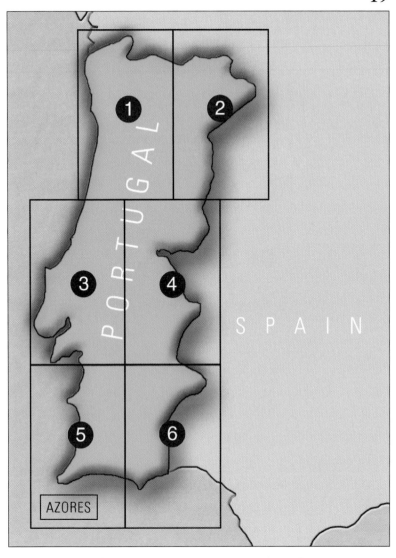

Guide to our map page numbers

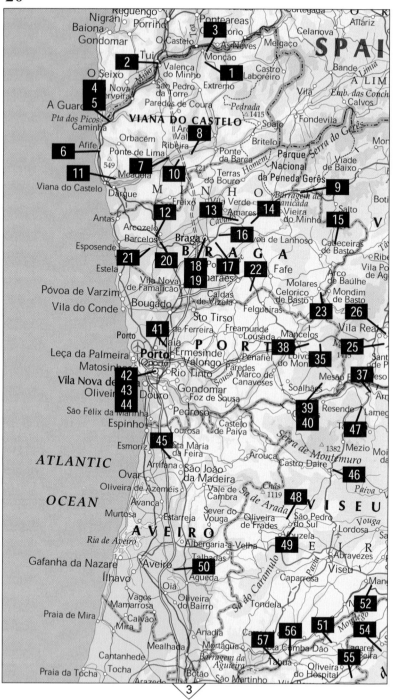

**Map 1**

©Bartholomew 1999

**Map 2**

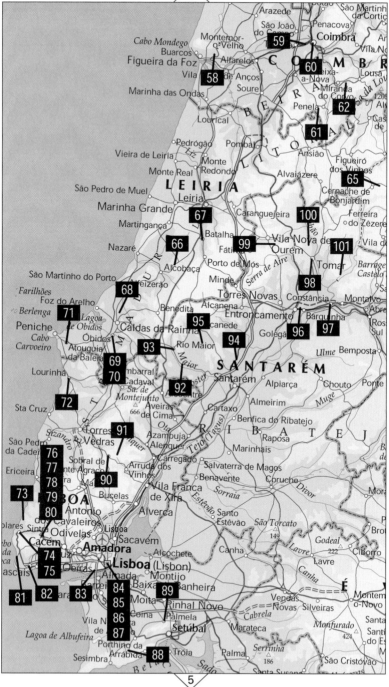

**Map 3**

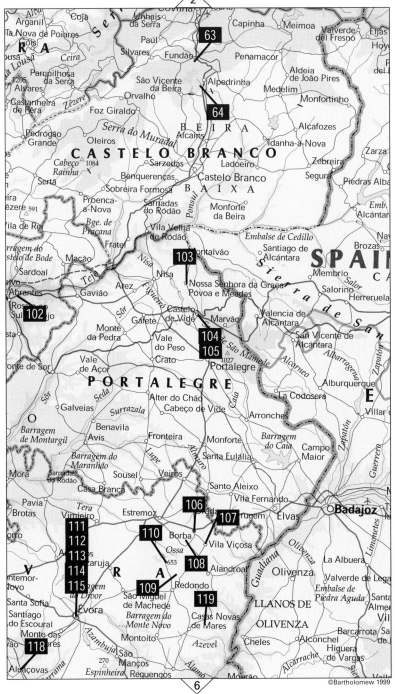

**Map 4**

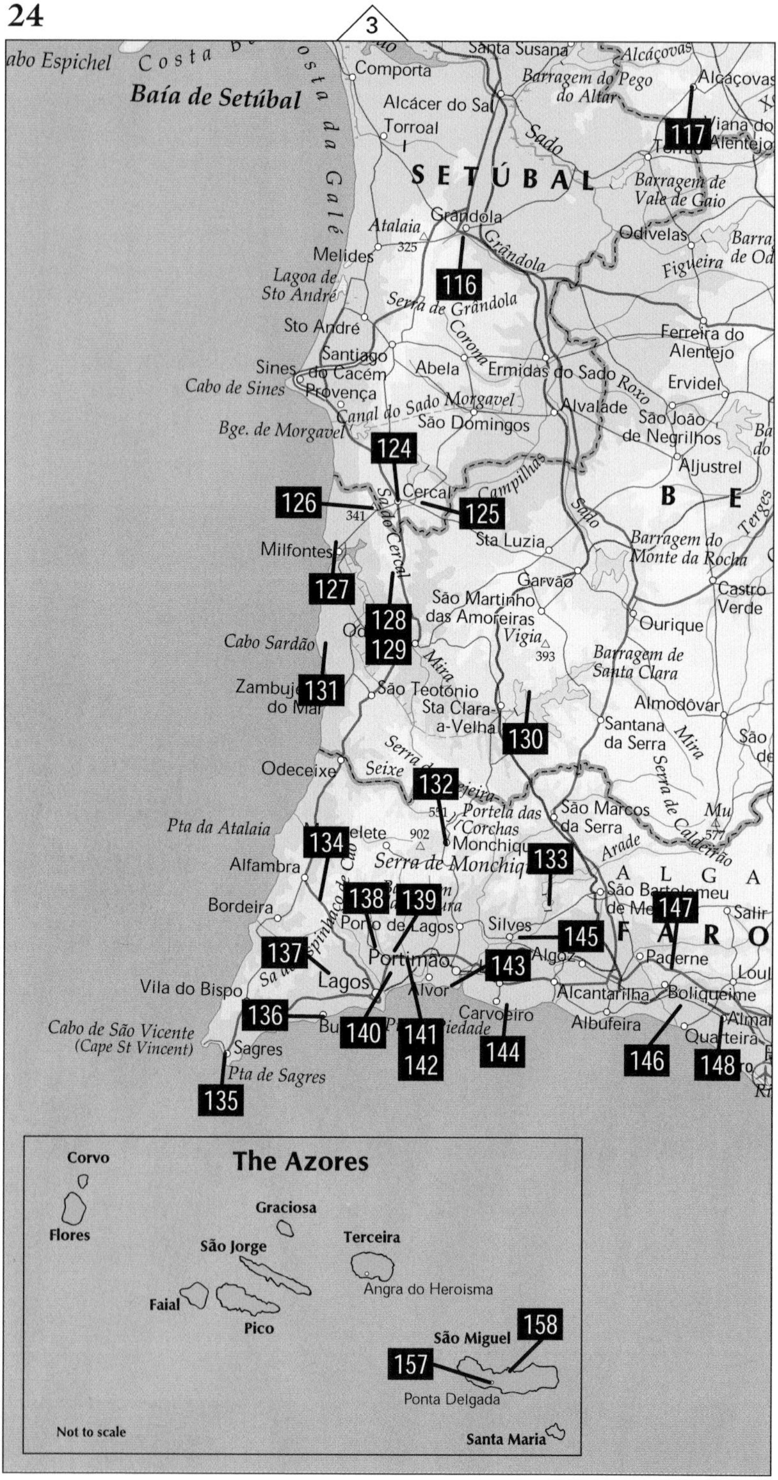

3

*Cabo Espichel* Costa *Comporta* Santa Susana *Alcáçovas* Alcáçovas

**Baía de Setúbal**

Alcácer do Sal
Torroal

*Barragem do Pego do Altar*

**117**

Viana do Alentejo

**SETÚBAL**

Grândola

*Sado*

*Barragem de Vale de Gaio*

Odivelas

*Barra de Od*

*Atalaia* 325

Melides

*Lagoa de Sto André*

*Serra de Grândola*

**116**

*Grândola*

Figueira

Ferreira do Alentejo

Sto André

Abela

Ermidas do Sado

Ervidel

Sines

Santiago do Cacém

Provença

*Cabo de Sines*

*Canal do Sado* Morgavel

São João de Negrilhos

Alvalade

*Bge. de Morgavel*

São Domingos

**124**

Aljustrel

**B E**

**126**

Cercal

*Campilhas*

341

**125**

Sta Luzia

*Terges*

Milfontes

Garvão

*Barragem do Monte da Rocha*

**127**

São Martinho das Amoreiras

*Vigia* 393

Ourique

Castro Verde

**128**
**129**

*Cabo Sardão*

*Mira*

*Barragem de Santa Clara*

Almodôvar

Zambuje do Mar

**131**

São Teotónio
Sta Clara-a-Velha

Santana da Serra

São de

**130**

Odeceixe

*Serra de*
*Seixe*

*Mira*

*Serra de Caldeirão*

*Pta da Atalaia*

**132**

*Portela das Corchas*

São Marcos da Serra

Mu 577

Alfambra

*902*

Monchique

*Serra de Monchique*

**133**

*Arade*

**A L G A**

Bordeira

**134**

**138** **139**

São Bartolomeu de Me

**147**

Salir

Porto de Lagos

Silves

**145**

**F A R O**

Paderne

**137**

Portimão

**143**

Algoz

Loul

Vila do Bispo

Lagos

Alvor

**146**

Boliqueime

Alma

*Cabo de São Vicente*
*(Cape St Vincent)*

**136**

Bu

**140**

**141**
**142**

Carvoeiro
*iedade*

**144**

Alcantarilha

Albufeira

Quarteira

**148**

Sagres

*Pta de Sagres*

**135**

---

### The Azores

Corvo

Graciosa

Flores

São Jorge

Terceira

Angra do Heroísma

Faial

Pico

São Miguel

**158**

**157**

Ponta Delgada

Not to scale

Santa Maria

---

**Map 5**

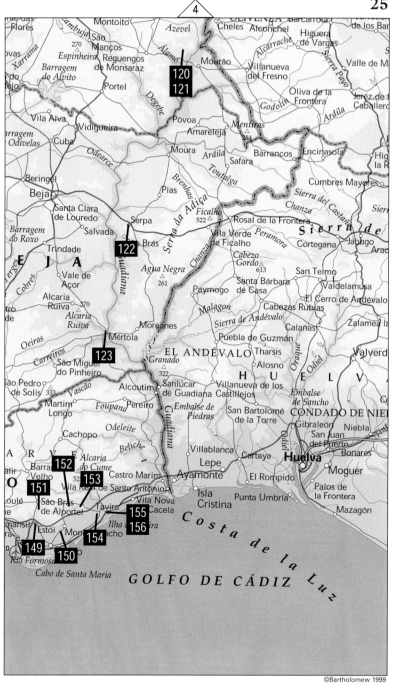

**Map 6**

Minho

•

Trás-os-Montes

•

Douro

# Northern Portugal

"If ever a decent excuse could be offered for perfect laziness, it was to
be found in the warm, enervating atmosphere, loaded with perfume,
which universally invested this pleasant umbragreous region."
William Beckford

# Casa de Rodas

4950 Monção                    **Tel:** 251 652105
Minho

**Maria Luisa Távora**

Casa de Rodas is certainly a sight for (city) sore eyes; a long sweep of lawn
bordering the main drive, then in the distance the low, clean-cut manor house with
its chapel grafted onto one flank. This impressive home has been in the family for
more than 400 years but don't expect your hosts to be pretentious about their
aristocratic lineage: Maria Luisa's casual manner and her genuine friendliness when
she greets you are a lovely appetiser for the experience of being here. There are a
number of reception rooms on the ground floor, each quite different from the
next; they have marvellous wooden ceilings, stucco and panelling, *trompe l'oeil*
marble and painted friezes. The overall effect is festive and fun. There are family
antiques, portraits and photos; masses of books and comfy sofas to read them in, a
grandfather clock, piano and games table. The bedrooms are just as memorable.
Each one is different, most vast and with its own dressing room. The newer rooms
are beautiful too and have bigger bathrooms and their own balconies but less of a
feel for the past. Our inspector purred "one of the most beautiful houses I've
visited... a knockout place".

**Rooms:** 10 with bath or shower & wc.
**Price:** Single Esc 11,600; Double/Twin
Esc 14,000.
**Breakfast:** Included.
**Meals:** None available.
**Closed:** Never.

From Valença, just after turn to Moncão,
turn right at Turismo de Habitação sign.
Gateway to Casa de Rodas after 200m.

**Map no:** 1                                   Entry no: 1

## Casa do Poço
Travessa da Gaviarra, 4
4930 Valença
Minho

**Tel:** 251 825235
**Fax:** 251 825469

Philippe Eckerle

Venture up into this fascinating citadel of Valença and stay a while at the Casa do Poço. The seductive cream façade raises expectations which are fully met inside. If you imagine that you're in an antique shop and art gallery, well you are, as all the furnishings and pictures are for sale. Where else would you be able to buy an original Turner or Picasso? Philippe is the essence of Gallic charm, which is reflected both in the look of the place and in his wonderful, imaginative cooking. The sitting and dining rooms are light and cheery and the parquet floors, chandeliers and liberal use of glass date from a complete restoration of the house. There's a well-stocked library, and in good weather the roof terrace is perfect at dusk for relaxation and a drink. But most of all you'll remember the Casa do Poço for its bedrooms, where silk-lined walls, antique lamps, original oils and carefully co-ordinated colours create an opulent mood. All help make this place special. Leave exploring the old town to the evening, when the day-trippers have gone and the old town can start to work its magic.

**Rooms:** 6 with bath & wc.
**Price:** Double Esc 15,000-20,000.
**Breakfast:** Included.
**Meals:** Dinner Esc 5,000, plus wine.
**Closed:** Never.

Arriving in Valença follow signs to Fortaleza. Pass through three gates in town walls, follow one-way system round cobbled streets and you'll see the façade.

# Solar de Serrade

Mazedo
4950-280 Monção
Minho

**Tel:** 251 65 40 08 / 649480
**Fax:** 251 65 40 41
**E-mail:** quintadeserrade@clix.pt
**Web:** planeta.clix.pt/QuintadeSerrade/

**Adriano Pereira Afonso**

This magnificent 17th-century Minho house, with its long sweep of façade and twin towers, is rich in history that stretches back to the 12th century. The Solar's last harvest produced 36,000 bottles of Alvarinho wine: it is Adriano's pride and joy and he'll encourage you to try a bottle or two should you come and stay at Serrade. As you enter the imposing entrance hall, with tiled walls, stone arches and ornate ceiling, you will marvel at the craftsmanship which is everywhere visible in stone, wood and tiles. Serrade's suite bedrooms are magnificent, with parquet floors, rugs, ornate four-poster beds, wooden ceilings and sufficient space to include a sofabed in the *sala*. The modern double bedrooms are smaller and cosier, with beautiful carved wooden beds and other stylish furniture; there are chandeliers and the swish bathrooms. On the ground floor there is a large breakfast room, formerly a bar, with attractive half-tiled walls and a sculpted ceiling. The dining room is big, too, with terracotta floors, high wooden ceilings and granite walls. There is a games room, a superb old chapel, and the chance to visit the impressive winery.

**Rooms:** 6 with bath & wc; 4 2-bed suites.
**Price:** Double/Twin Esc 8,000-12,000; Single Esc 8,000-12,000; Suites Esc 12,000-18,000.
**Breakfast:** Included.
**Meals:** Lunch/Dinner by arrangement, Esc 3,000.
**Closed:** Never.

Heading south on the N101 from Monção, cross the N202, go a further 200m and turn left (east) to Sago. The Solar is 1km along this road.

**Map no: 1**

# Quinta da Graça
4910-608 Caminha        **Tel:** 258 921157/22 609 0751
Minho

**Maria Helena Pacheco de Amorim**

The pretty town of Caminha hugs the southern bank of the Minho where it meets the Atlantic; the town's fortifications speak of an age when this was an important frontier post between Portugal and Spain. Close by are some of the country's loveliest beaches and, cradled on a hillside of the Coura Valley with heavenly views down to the estuary and sea beyond, is the Quinta da Graça. This elegantly mannered farmhouse dates from the 17th century, and ivy, flowered borders and a statue of the Virgin grace the façade. We loved the guest rooms and apartments (in the old servants' quarters); most have period furniture – some of it locally crafted, some the more exotic Indo-Portuguese style – and one bedroom has Victorian furniture. Old hand-painted tiles in the bathrooms (some with baths, others shower) are works of art. You breakfast at a heavy chestnut table in the old rustic kitchen. After your meal wander through Graca's peaceful garden, take a pool-side seat overlooking river and valley, or settle down in the tome-filled library. Apartments have their own kitchenette and are more simply furnished. There are restaurants for all budgets close by. *Your host speaks French and Spanish.*

**Rooms:** 7 with bath & wc; 1 suite and 1 apartment.
**Price:** Double/Twin Esc 15,000; Suite Esc 18,000; Apartment 15,000.
Extra bed Esc 3500.
**Breakfast:** Included.
**Meals:** None available.
**Closed:** Easter & Christmas.

From Porto IC1 to Viana do Castelo then towards Valença to Caminha. There, to centre, right to main square with fountain. Then 2nd left up hill towards fortress. House just after sign 'Miradouro', close to block of flats.

Entry no: 4        Map no: 1

# Casa de Esteiró

Vilarelho
4910-605 Caminha
Minho

**Tel:** 258 721333
**Fax:** 258 921356

### José Manuel Villas-Boas

A magical old house which reflects the warm, outgoing personalities of owners José and Maria, the Casa de Esteiró is a rich experience from the moment you pass under the rugged stone archway. This late 18th-century house is extremely handsome and decorated with antiques and fine furniture; traditional Portuguese and finds from the owners' years abroad in the diplomatic service. The gallery is long, with masses of comfortable seating, beautiful cushions, porcelain and paintings, plus a lovely, granite fireplace. The library is exquisite, and there is a small chapel off it (ask about the altar carried by the great-grandfather during the Peninsular War). The bedrooms too have both Portuguese and foreign furnishings. The self-catering apartments have their own living rooms, but guests are also welcome in the main house. Breakfast is served either in the bedrooms or in the huge dining room, lined with beautiful ceramic dishes. Outside there is a good pool and a garden with many specimen trees (planted by an earlier owner, Viscount Negrelos), which thrive in this Minho climate. There are quiet areas for sitting and listening to the running water and birds.

**Rooms:** 8 with bath & wc.
**Price:** Double/Twin Esc 13,000; Single Esc 10,000; Apartment (for 4) Esc 24,000, (for 2) Esc 13,000.
**Breakfast:** Included.
**Meals:** None available.
**Closed:** Never.

Follow Viana do Castelo road to Valença on N13. Arrive in Caminha, turn right at sign for Centre & Turismo de Habitação. After 50m, right at sign Casa de Esteiró.

**Map no:** 1

Entry no: 5

# Casa Santa Filomena

Estrada de Cabanas
Afife
4900-012 Viana do Castelo
Minho

**Tel:** 258 981619 or 22 6174161/2
**Fax:** 22 6175936
**E-mail:** soc.com.smiths@mail.telepac.pt

### José Street Kendall

A grand entrance gate beckons you in to the Casa Santa Filomena, a solid, stonewalled building that was built in the 1920s. It is hidden away in a quiet corner of an already quiet village; your rest is assured. When we visited in early spring the old wisteria was a riot of tumbling lilac and mauve, as pretty a welcome as you could wish for. A high wall runs round the property; it girdles a small vineyard where *vinho verde* grapes are grown. Elsewhere the profusion of flowers is heady proof of the microclimate that this part of the Minho enjoys; it seems as if anything will grow here. The rooms are rather functional but perfectly clean and comfortable. If staying here, do have dinner in; much of your meal will have been grown in Filomena's garden and this is the occasion to try the estate's lovely wine. If there's anything that you'd especially like to eat – just tell José. A delightful, secluded spot – and very good value. And, among other diversions, a swimming pool and tennis courts are just a kilometre away.

**Rooms:** 4 with bath & wc; 1 suite.
**Price:** Double/Twin Esc 13,000;
Apartment Esc 20,000.
**Breakfast:** Included.
**Meals:** Lunch/dinner on request, Esc 2,500-3,500.
**Closed:** Never.

From Valença to Viana second left to Afife. From Viana first right. When you reach the centre of Afife turn inland (Estrada de Cabanas). The house is 800m from the first junction.

Entry no: 6                Map no: 1

# Paço de Calheiros

Calheiros
4990 Ponte de Lima
Minho

**Tel:** 258 947164
**Fax:** 258 947294
**E-mail:** paco_calheiros@nortenet.pt

### Francisco, Conde de Calheiros

You feel you should be arriving by horse and carriage as you pass through the wrought-iron gates, along the drive lined with plane trees and past the vineyards and fountain. And there to greet you is the gracious twin-towered and ivy-clad façade; a staircase leads up to the sculpted portal of the main entrance. The family has lived here for over six and a half centuries. The house was rebuilt in the 17th century but the Calheiros have stayed resolutely at the helm; it was the charming Francisco, present Count of Calheiros, who opened the house to all. Inside, everything lives up to expectations. There are several *salons* brimming with antiques, all with large stone hearths, and in one of the dining rooms is a 10-metre-long table which can seat 30. Choose between self-catering apartments or the grandest of doubles in the main house; all of them have period furnishing and they're large enough for a waltz. But leave time to wander the exquisite formal gardens or saddle up a horse and ride the estate. The swimming pool has a glorious view and there's a tennis court, too.

**Rooms:** 9 with bath & wc, plus 6 apartments.
**Price:** Double/Twin Esc 20,000; Apartment Esc 20,000.
**Breakfast:** Included.
**Meals:** Occasionally available Esc 6,000.
**Closed:** Never.

From Braga on the N201 to Ponte de Lima. Here, cross the river and after petrol station right towards Arcos de Valdevez/Valença. After 1km, right towards Arcos, then after 4km, left towards Calheiros. On right after 2km.

**Map no: 1**

Entry no: 7

# Casa da Várzea

Várzea
Beiral do Lima
4990-545 Ponte de Lima
Minho

**Tel:** 258 948603
**Fax:** 258 948412
**E-mail:** casa.varzea@netc.pt

**Ináçio Barreto Caldas da Costa**

You'll see Casa da Várzea as you wind your way up from the valley below. It would be hard not to fall in love with the beauty of the place, cradled among terraced vineyards. Like so many of the grand old homes of Portugal it lay abandoned for many years, but Inácio Caldas da Costa, whose feelings ran deep for the house where he was born, took courage and after his retirement set about the restoration of the family seat. Várzea now has six big, light and charmingly decorated rooms, and Inaçio and his wife are warm and welcoming hosts. Family antiques are here for you to enjoy; you may find yourself in grandmother's or great-uncle's bed, made in cherry. Bedrooms are large and cool, and one has a lovely old Minho chest with a secret drawer for hiding gold sovereigns. Prints and framed embroidery, polished wooden floors and rugs are endearingly domestic. And in the public rooms wood-clad floors and ceilings lend warmth to grandeur. At breakfast there are long views from the airy dining room, plus home-made jams and fruit from the farm. There's a library, a pool with-a-view and the old wooden 'drying house', now a second lounge/playroom. And a bar for tasting local *vinho verde*.

**Rooms:** 6 with bath & wc.
**Price:** Single Esc 12,500; Double/Twin Esc 15,000.
**Breakfast:** Included.
**Meals:** Dinner (usually fish) on request Esc 2,500.
**Closed:** Never.

From Porto-Valença dual carriageway exit for Ponte da Barca. Continue for 6km to S. Martinho Gandra. Here right to Beiral.
100m past church turn right at stone cross. Along this lane to house.

Entry no: 8

Map no: 1

# Casa de Dentro 'Capitão – Mor'

Vila-Ruivães                          **Tel:** 253 658117
C.180                                 **Fax:** 253 658117
4850-341 Vieira do Minho              **E-mail:** ammf2000@clix.pt
Minho

### Ilda de Jesus Truta Fraga de Miranda Fernandes

This was once the home of none other than Capitão-Mor de Ruivães who put the French to rout during the Peninsular War (the 'War of Independence' to the Portuguese). It sits proudly on one side of the valley which divides the Cabeira and Gerês mountain ranges in the tiniest of hamlets amid the terraced vineyards and deep greenery of the Minho. Both hosts and home exude warmth and welcome. Ilda, a retired school teacher, relishes in sharing her intimate knowledge of this corner of the Minho – she has maps ready for your walks and will tell you about the region's fascinating mythology. We loved the sitting room with its low beams, granite hearth, old copper still and wall cabinets displaying the family china – just the place for settling down with a good book. The guest rooms are as unassuming as the rest of Ilda's home: they vary in size but all have antique beds and wardrobes, parquet floors, rugs and pretty bedside lamps. Breakfast is as generous as Ilda herself: yoghurts, home-made jams, fruit juice and very special cake, Ilda's *bola de carne folar* (visit to discover the secret!). There is a tennis court, pool-with-a-view and the wonderful Gerês Park right on your doorstep.

**Rooms:** 5 with bath & wc; 1 apartment for 6.
**Price:** Double/Twin Esc 12,500; Single Esc 10,000; Apt. (for 6) Esc 200,000 per week.
**Breakfast:** Included.
**Meals:** None available.
**Closed:** Never.

From Braga take EN103 for 42km to Ruivães. House is in centre of village to right of church.

**Map no: 1**                         Entry no: 9

# Casa de Pomarchão

Arcozelo
4990-068 Ponte de Lima
Minho

**Tel:** 258 741742 or 91 720 4615 (mob)
**Fax:** 258 742742

**Frederico Villar**

Casa de Pomarchão dates all the way back to the 15th century but owes its present look to a rebuild of 1775 when a Baroque chapel and veranda were added. The manor is at the centre of a 60-hectare estate of vineyards and thick pine forest. Your choice is between an apartment in the wonderful main building (every inch the aristocrat's residence) or your own solidly built house. Some are classical in style (*Milho,* and *Bica*), others have a more rustic feel (*Toca* and *Mato*). What is so refreshing is their utter comfort; no corners have been cut. The houses all have hearths, top-quality sofas, warm curtains, paintings, good beds and well-equipped kitchens. French windows take you out to your own garden or terrace and the whole of the estate is yours for the walking. You can swim in the huge old water tank, visit nearby Ponte de Lima and the beach is just a short drive away. This is a wonderful place to head for if you are planning a longer stay in Portugal. Frederico's wife greets you with a smile; she speaks excellent English. You'll be loathe to pack your suitcase and to say goodbye to (we quote our inspector) "the biggest, softest dog I have ever seen".

**Rooms:** 10 self-catering apartments and houses with bath or shower & wc.
**Price:** Double/Twin Esc 12,000 for 2. Prices for larger apartments/houses on request.
**Breakfast:** Included.
**Meals:** None available.
**Closed:** December 10-30.

2km outside Ponte de Lima on road to Valença N201. Signposted.

Entry no: 10

Map no: 1

# Casa do Ameal

Rua do Ameal, 119          **Tel:** 258 822403
Meadela
4900-204 Viana do Castelo
Minho

**Maria Elisa de Magalhães Faria Araújo**

Although it has now been absorbed into the urban fabric of Viana, once you pass into the entrance courtyard of Casa do Ameal, with its box hedges and gurgling fountain, you can leave the outside world behind. It was bought in 1669 by the de Faria Araújo family whose numerous descendants still watch over the place; there are 14 siblings in the present generation and five of the sisters still live at the house (most of the others arrive at the weekend!). These loveable elderly ladies welcome you with tea and a tour of the house; they will proudly show off the collection of handicrafts and the family costume 'museum' with such delights as their grandparents' christening robes. Accommodation is in two guest rooms and seven apartments, some sleeping two, others four; most have their own kitchenette. The rooms are furnished in a simple, rustic style that goes well with the exposed stone walls. The sisters speak English, French and Spanish and will gladly help you plan your excursions to Viana do Castelo, where there are good restaurants, just two kilometres away.

**Rooms:** 2 doubles & 7 apartments (for 2 or 4).
**Price:** Single Esc 11,600; Double 14,000; Apartment (for 2) Esc 14,000, (for 4) Esc 22,400.
**Breakfast:** Included.
**Meals:** On request for large groups or self-catering.
**Closed:** Never.

From Porto take the N13/IC1 towards Viana do Castelo. Just before Viana enter village Meadela, pass main square, church and drive on until big supermarket 'Continente'. Turn left as if to go to supermarket, but pass their parking, drive up the hill and turn left at gates to the house.

**Map no:** 1                                           Entry no: 11

# Casa do Monte

Lugar do Barreiro
Abade de Neiva
4750 Barcelos
Minho

**Tel:** 253 811519
**Fax:** 253 811519

### Maria do Rosário Sousa Coutinho

The house stands proud on a hillside in a tiny hamlet looking out across the green valley of Barcelos. The main drive cuts an arc upwards past carefully clipped hedges of box, enormous camellias, a statue and a ceramic plaque; it praises God for blessing the Minho with places as heavenly as this. Come if only to see these pampered gardens. The house is a well-mannered building which you might well imagine to be older than its 60 years; light granite lintels, bright sky-blue window frames and *azulejos* give the façade a merry air. And the gaiety is mirrored inside the house; bright primary colours decorate panelling, skirting, chairs and tables in the unforgettable dining room. In the bedrooms the same idea adds cheer to radiators and window seats, beds and wardrobes. We marginally preferred those on the first floor but those giving onto the lower terrace are special too – and all rooms have views across the valley. In among the carefully clipped hedges are a pool and tennis court, but your attention will first be caught by the profusion of shrubs, trees and flowers; this is one of the loveliest gardens of northern Portugal. Try to catch the Thursday market in Barcelos.

**Rooms:** 6 with bath & wc.
**Price:** Single Esc 9,000; Double/Twin Esc 12,000.
**Breakfast:** Included.
**Meals:** None available.
**Closed:** November-April

From Barcelos take old road to Viana do Castelo. After 4km you arrive in hamlet of Abade de Neiva; Casa do Monte on right.

Entry no: 12

Map no: 1

# Casa São Vicente

Lugar de Portas
Geraz do Minho
4830-315 Póvoa do Lanhoso
Minho

**Tel:** 253 632466
**Fax:** 253 632466

**Teresa V Ferreira**

This is an address ideal for those who love the grape, for the Minho's delightful *vinho verde* is produced here and you can visit and buy from the *adega* (the 'green', incidentally, refers to age not colour). Teresa and her husband will share much more wine-talk should you stay with them at this old bougainvillaea-clad farmhouse. This is a relaxed sort of place: solidly comfortable and not a bit ostentatious. An enormous drawing room feels more like a conservatory with high windows opening on two sides, with family photos, a woodburner and plenty of sofa space. The dining room is off to one end; at breakfast, expect a big spread and a chance to admire the large collection of porcelain. In warmer weather you will eat out under the orange trees with a view of the vineyards. And your sleep should be deep; bedrooms are manicured, large and light. *Cor de Rosa* has its own veranda, *Amerelo* would be perfect for a family, *Azul* is rather smaller but pretty just the same. Ask to be shown the unusual paintings in the Quinta's chapel (1623) and find time to visit the diminutive castle of nearby Póvoa do Lanhoso.

**Rooms:** 5 with bath or shower & wc;
1 small house.
**Price:** Double/Twin Esc 12,000; 2-bed house Esc 12,000 for two; Esc 24,000 for four.
**Breakfast:** Included.
**Meals:** Light lunch & dinner on request, Esc 2,000, inc. wine.
**Closed:** Never.

From Porto take the A3, exit to Braga and here towards Chaves to Arcas. Towards Amares then after 1.5km turn left for Geras/Ferreiros/Covelas. Signposted.

**Map no: 1**

**Entry no: 13**

# Casa de Requeixo

Frades
4830-216 Póvoa do Lanhoso
Minho

**Tel:** 253 631112
**Fax:** 253 636499

**Maria Henriqueta Norton**

The Baron of São Roque's house has been in the same family since it was built in 1513 by Vicente Gil, owner of the sailing ship *Nossa Senhora da Graça*. Not surprisingly, every room has a story to tell, and the friendly, well educated owners Maria and Manuel Artur, (the English surname dates back to the 18th century port wine trade) will be pleased to share some of them over a cup of coffee. In the breakfast room, once the old kitchen, is the family's coat of arms on a shield. Despite Napoleon's troops burning the house during the Peninsular War in 1809, there is much to see – including the 18th-century chapel and its gilded altar. The front of the house is 17th century, the back, with its large stones visible, is original 16th century. Inside this venerable edifice the sitting room is large and comfortable with old oils on the walls and a mixture of antique and rustic furniture. Bedrooms have the same mix of styles and beds are *Dona Maria* and Dom João V – very impressive – with views of the farm and surrounding countryside. There's a well-equipped private kitchen for guests, too, and numerous restaurants nearby.

**Rooms:** 2 with bath & wc, 2 with shower & wc and 2 apartments.
**Price:** Double/Twin Esc 10,000; Apartment Esc 10,000.
**Breakfast:** Included; apartment self-catering.
**Meals:** None available.
**Closed:** Never.

From Braga, 16km along the N103 towards Chaves, turn right at sign to Frades; take right fork in Frades and continue. The house is on the left shortly before the Church of S. António.

# Casa de Canêdo

Barreiro CP 101
4890-140 Celorico de Basto
Minho

**Tel:** 255 361293
**Fax:** 255 361765

**Maria José Silva**

The setting for this 17th-century manor is superb: in a peaceful valley amid vineyards, forested hills and mountains. The new wing (early 19th century) is in granite, the older part rendered in earthy yellow. The centuries live side by side here and bedrooms and suites are all different: the Romantic room has a great mahogany double bed and looks over fields; the *Cameleiras* suite has a large sitting room and opens to a garden of camellias; the *Quarto das Laranjeiras* leads to an orange grove. The *Chapel* room has *Dona Maria* twins and the *Patio* room, which opens onto the inner courtyard and fountain, D. João V furniture. All have something special and the Senhora da Graça mountain is seen from several bedrooms. The large lounge has plenty of sofas, a granite fireplace and an 18th-century oil of Our Lady; in the *Piano Room* there is a 19th-century grand and old portraits. The dining room is wonderfully rustic, with long wooden table and fireplace, walls and floor of granite. Outside are gardens and 90 acres of vineyards; the cellars are still used for the Casa de Canêdo *vinho verde* – excellent with the good Minho cooking; most of the food and juices are fresh from the farm.

**Rooms:** 6 with bath & wc; 3 suites.
**Price:** Double/Twin Esc 15,000; Single Esc 12,500; Suite Esc 15,000; (2 people) Esc 18,500, (3 people) Esc 20,000.
**Breakfast:** Included.
**Meals:** Lunch/dinner available with notice, Esc 3,500.
**Closed:** December 15-January 15.

On the EN205 Cabaceiras de Basto-Amarante road, between the villages of Arco de Baúlhe and Fermil de Basto, look for signs to the house.

**Map no: 1**

Entry no: 15

# Castelo de Bom Jesus

Bom Jesus
4710-455 Braga
Minho

**Tel:** 253 676566
**Fax:** 253 677691
**E-mail:** charmhotelsmail.telepac.pt
**Web:** www.castelo-bom-jesus.com

### Dr Manuel de Castro Meirelles

The Castelo do Bom Jesus looks down over the city of Braga and all the way to the Atlantic coast. Enter beneath the grand portal sculpted with the family coat of arms. The blue-blooded Meirelles, part of the House of Bragança, have lived here since an ancestor built this grandest of homes in the 18th century. The outside was remodelled in the Neo-Gothic style by Swiss architect Korrodi and has the mixed-style fantasy of the Rhine Castles; the present generation of the Meirelles restored the interiors. Rooms are as sumptuous as you'd expect, with regal beds; the presidential suite is the grandest, with *trompe l'oeil* frescoes, period furniture and jacuzzi. (Suites have air-conditioning.) Continental breakfast is served at a huge dining table in a graceful room beneath family portraits; dress for dinner in the oval, chandeliered dining room with its beautiful wrap-around fresco of arches and fabulous gardens. In the long lounge are grand piano and harp; a second salon is given over to the billiard table. And the gardens! Abandon yourself to an oasis of green and calm where peacocks roam. Wind your way past exotic plants and trees via a grotto and on up to the views from the belvedere.

**Rooms:** 11 with bath & wc & 2 suites.
**Price:** Double 'Standard' Esc 15,000;
Double 'Superior' Esc 25,000;
Suite Esc 35,000.
**Breakfast:** Included.
**Meals:** Lunch/dinner Esc 4,000-5,000.
**Closed:** Never.

From Porto A3-IP then N14 to Braga. Here follow signs for Bom Jesus to top of the hill; right through gate just before Sanctuary car park.

Entry no: 16

Map no: 1

# Casa dos Lagos
Bom Jesus
4710-455 Braga
Minho

**Tel:** 253 676738
**Fax:** 253 679207
**E-mail:** casadoslagosbomjesus@oninet.pt

**Andrelina Pinto Barbosa**

A warm, dignified welcome awaits you at Casa dos Lagos. The house was built by a viscount at the end of the 18th century on a wooded hillside which it shares with the Bom Jesus sanctuary; don't miss the extraordinary Baroque staircase which zigzags up to the chapel on top of the hill, but do visit on a weekday to avoid the crowds of pilgrims. Both the devout and not so devout are welcome at Andrelina's home which is a lesson in quiet elegance. Light floods in through the French windows of the sitting/dining room; at one end there is a drop-leaf table beneath a fine chandelier (there will be cake for breakfast), and at the other is a velvet sofa drawn up to a large fireplace where you may sip a pre-dinner glass of port served from a cut-glass decanter. The terrace gives onto a garden where stands of camellias break up the order of carefully clipped box hedges and ornamental fountains; the views from here are breathtaking. Only one bedroom is in the main house. It is large, elegantly corniced and has a fine antique bedroom set: marble-topped dresser, cavernous wardrobe and ornately carved bed. Other rooms and the apartments are more modern and these, too, are large and well-equipped.

**Rooms:** 3 with bath & wc; 4 apartments.
**Price:** Double/Twin Esc 15,000; Apartment (for 2) Esc 15,000, (for 4) Esc 24,000.
**Breakfast:** Included.
**Meals:** None available.
**Closed:** Never.

From Braga take EN103 to Bom Jesus. Here, turn right at signs.

# Hotel do Elévador

Monte do Bom Jesus
4710-455 Braga
Minho

**Tel:** 253 603400
**Fax:** 253 603409
**E-mail:** hoteisbomjesus@hoteisbomjesus.web.pt
**Web:** www.hoteisbomjesus.web.pt

**Albino Viana**

Pilgrims climb the wooded hillside of Bom Jesus to the church via a famous zig-zag Baroque staircase. If your legs give way you can proceed on your knees, take the funicular elevator, or pause to think. Close at hand is the four-star Hotel do Elevador, which takes its name from a water-powered 19th-century lift. The long-fronted, classically Portuguese building was superbly restored in 1998, and you will be cosseted. There are marble floors, beautiful rugs and silk wallpaper, a combination of Portuguese tradition and modern style. Bedrooms are big, elegantly furnished with ornate wooden beds and fine fabrics; bathrooms have marble floors. The suites, with their big living rooms, are similar in style. All but four rooms have views of the park and Braga below. In the large sitting room you can relax on sand and blue sofas. The restaurant offers regional and traditional cooking, and local dishes include Braga duck and roasted kid. Local wines are well worth sampling and there is also a large panoramic restaurant, much enjoyed by the locals. Fortified by good Minho food and wine, you won't find that climb half as daunting...

**Rooms:** 22 with bath & wc.
**Price:** Double/Twin Esc 13,800-17,000; Single Esc 10,900-13,900.
**Breakfast:** Included.
**Meals:** Lunch Esc 3,000-3,500; dinner à la carte also available.
**Closed:** Never.

Upon entering Braga, at the main roundabout follow signs to Chaves and the Universidade do Minho. At the top of the main Avenida João XXI turn right for Hotéis do Bom Jesus.

Entry no: 18          Map no: 1

# Hotel do Parque

Monte do Bom Jesus
4710-455 Braga
Minho

**Tel:** 253 603470
**Fax:** 253 603479
**E-mail:** hoteisbomjesus@hoteisbomjesus.web.pt
**Web:** www.hoteisbomjesus.web.pt

**Albino Viana**

Large and luxurious, this is the big sister hotel to the Hotel do Elevador [entry 18], only a few yards away. It is a large square building on four floors, elegant, and furnished to a very high standard. As you walk through the foyer you'll find the atmosphere professional and smooth-running rather than homely, but staff are very courteous and there are plenty of places to relax. The bedrooms and suites, which have views of the gardens, are traditional in style, with high-quality reproduction furniture and good covers and curtains. Buffet-style breakfast is generous and guests should try the neighbouring Elevador's restaurant. Otherwise, you can relax in the comfortable bar and lounge, the latter with a fireplace, enjoy the games room (there are tennis courts nearby), and of course the surrounding gardens, with their pools, trimmed lawns and luxuriant plants. There are also two interior winter gardens (too hot in the summer). Such is the appeal of the pilgrimage walk that the hotel has guests all year round. A great time to visit is during the festival of St. John in late June, when the whole of Braga parties for nights on end. You'll be glad to get back to your room!

**Rooms:** 42 all with bath & wc, 3 triples and 4 suites.
**Price:** Double/Twin Esc 13,800-17,000; Single Esc 10,900-13,900; Suite Esc 14,500-20,000.
**Breakfast:** Included
**Meals:** Lunch/Dinner, Esc 3,000-3,500 plus wine; also packed lunches.
**Closed:** Never.

Upon entering Braga, at the main roundabout follow signs to Chaves and the Universidade do Minho; at the top of the main Avenida João XXI turn right for Hotéis do Bom Jesus.

**Map no: 1**

Entry no: 19

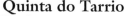

# Quinta do Tarrio

Tamel
Santa Leocárdia
4750 Barcelos
Minho

**Tel:** 253 88 1558
**Fax:** 253 88 2773

### Marine & George Ennis

A farm with 300 years of history, this delightful place sits in gardens of lawns, flowers, orange, lemon, pear and plum trees and is surrounded by vineyards and a kiwi plantation. Owners Marine, who is Swedish, and George, who spent much of his early life in Norway, are informal and welcoming. They will show you the farm's *adega* where the famous local *vinho verde* is produced – well worth visiting for a tasting. The farmhouse is full of interesting antiques and ancient farming artefacts and has lots of space; guests can relax in the *sala*, a room of tile floors and rugs, with splendid views over the garden, orchards and beyond. In colder weather there are open log fires and woodburning stoves are lit. Guest rooms and their beds are large, (twin beds are zipped together to make doubles), comfortable and quiet with pretty curtains and cushions. Everything here is on a grand scale, not least the breakfasts; the juice comes from the estate-grown oranges and the home-made jams include kiwi. The grounds are full of variety, there's an attractive pool area, tennis court and space to play handball, volleyball and basketball. *Minimum stay 3 days.*

**Rooms:** 4 with shower or bath & wc, plus 2-bed suite.
**Price:** Double/Twin Esc 16,000;
Suite (for 2) Esc 16,000,
(for 4) Esc 22,000.
**Breakfast:** Included.
**Meals:** None available.
**Closed:** November-April.

From the IC1 look for Barcelos-Braga sign, then follow N205 until N103, then turn twice heading for Viana do Castelo, until a roundabout; go another 50m and take right to Tamel Sta. Leocárdia. 1km to Quinta.

# Quinta do Convento da Franqueira

Carvalhal CC 301
Franqueira
4755-104 Barcelos
Minho

**Tel:** 253 831606/831853
**Fax:** 253 832231

**Piers & Kate Gallie**

This wonderful 16th-century monastery is hidden away among pine trees, cork oaks, eucalyptus and cypress. It is rich in history, and the cloister is thought to have been built with stones from the ruins of the castle of Faria. Certainly the brothers came here for the splendid isolation and spring which now feeds a swimming pool, built above ornamental steps and with excellent views of house and church. Five centuries on, the granite buildings have been restored to their former grace by the Gallie family; a labour of love for 'how things were'; the results are deeply pleasing. Rooms and suite are lovely, of generous proportions and furnished with fine antiques. There's a four-poster in one room, old prints, pretty bedside lamps and tables and stuccoed ceilings; all are individual. Bathrooms have hand-painted tiles. The estate produces its own *vinho verde* from vineyards that roll right up to Franqueira's walls; Piers Gallie enjoys showing guests round the winery. Children will enjoy swings, gardens and the rocking horse in the play room; a huge tiled terrace overlooks lush gardens. Try to see the Thursday market in nearby Barcelos.

**Rooms:** 4 with bath & wc; 1 suite.
**Price:** Double/Twin Esc 13,000; Apartment Esc 20,000.
**Breakfast:** Included.
**Meals:** Occasionally available, approx. 4,500 Esc.
**Closed:** November-May.

From Braga N103 to Barcelos; at end of N103 right round ring road. Pass Renault garage then 2nd right towards Póvoa de Varzim. Under bridge then left to Franqueira. Through village; take middle road of three up hill into woods to bar. Here right, pass church and left through gates.

**Map no: 1**

# Quinta de Cima de Eiriz

Calvos
4810-605 Guimarães
Minho

**Tel:** 253 541750
**Fax:** 253 420559

**Dr. João Gaspar de Sousa Gomes Alves**

On a south-facing slope of the beautiful Penha mountain this old Minho Quinta has been completely restored. In the beamed and terracotta-tiled lounge, the old grape press has been transformed into an unusual raised bar. Marvel at the size of the granite lintels, flagstones and building blocks of the entrance hall. The pillar-box red of the doors and windows lends a lighter note. Bedrooms are in the old stable blocks, updated with central heating and phones and have sparkling marbled and tiled bathrooms. Most memorable are their views over the well-trimmed lawns and across the valley. Breakfast is a big meal; expect fresh orange juice, yoghurts, several types of bread and cake and Maria Adelaide's jams. Afterwards you could walk straight out to explore the Penha National Park. In the warmer months plunge into the pool or try the excellent games room; the balconied terrace is just right for a sun-downer; the views are long and rural. 10km away is Guimarães with narrow streets, castle and superb municipal museum, while closer still is the Santa Marinha da Costa Monastery, the best preserved medieval building of the region.

**Rooms:** 4 with bath & wc.
**Price:** Double/Twin Esc 13,000;
Apartment Esc 20,000.
**Breakfast:** Included.
**Meals:** None available.
**Closed:** Never.

Take autoroute Porto-Braga A3. In Vila Nova de Famalaicão take A7 to Guimarães. There take road towards Fafe/Felgueiras. After 4km right towards Felgueiras. After another 4km right at sign Penha/Lapinha (don't take first turn Penha/Calvos). After 2km left at a stone cross; signposted.

Entry no: 22

Map no: 1

# Casa do Campo

Molares
4890 Celorico de Basto
Minho

**Tel:** 255 361231
**Fax:** 255 361231

**Maria Armanda Meireles**

The Casa do Campo is every inch the classic *solar* or country manor. An enormous, ornately-sculpted portal and turreted outer wall protect the inner courtyard. The prize-winning formal gardens (which include an excellent swimming pool) are a hymn to the camellia – the country's oldest is said to be here and, thanks to careful topiary, they take on fabulous forms. The Meireles family has been here for centuries farming the estate and its vines. The art of receiving guests comes naturally to gracious Maria Armanda. Her guest bedrooms are in a renovated wing and are of the sort that we love; no two are the same, they are decorated in classical style and have polished wooden floors, elegantly stuccoed ceilings, cut flowers and a feeling of space. Breakfast in the classically elegant dining room with its beautiful paintings, cabinets of fine porcelain and carved ceiling; or there is a smaller, less formal dining room. Settle into the sitting room with its velvet chairs and old harpsichord or into the dream of a library with its tomes on the gardens of Portugal; Casa do Campo is featured in them all, of course. The manor's splendid Renaissance chapel still has a weekly mass.

**Rooms:** 7 with bath & wc; 1 suite.
**Price:** Single Esc 12,500; Double Esc 15,000; Suite approx. Esc 20,000.
**Breakfast:** Included.
**Meals:** Lunch/Dinner on request, approx. Esc 4,500.
**Closed:** Christmas.

From Braga N101 to Guimarães then N206 towards Fafe and Celorico de Basto/Mondim. At Gandarela right onto N304 to Fermil; here right onto N210 towards Celorico. Signposted after 1.5km.

**Map no: 1**

Entry no: 23

# Quinta do Barreiro

Guiães
Paredela de Guiães
5060 Vila Real
Trás-os-Montes

**Tel:** 254 920479 (booking: 259 323121)
**Fax:** 259 326553
**E-mail:** casa.mateus@utad.pt

**Fernando Albuquerque**

If you want to spend time away from the world come here. This restored 18th-century villa farmhouse is on top of a hill at the heart of the Douro valley surrounded by 40 hectares of terraced vineyards. There are vineyards as far as the eye can see and a pool that overlooks the valley. In spite of its isolation the house has every creature comfort: central heating, open hearths, and an enormous sitting room with a great table on granite supports, stone walls and panelled ceiling. The bedrooms have wooden floors, rugs and good quality furniture, and are light, fresh and with exceptional views. Your resident housekeepers, Sergio and Deolinda, will look after your every need, and shop for you if you wish; meals with regional food can be provided with notice. If renting the whole house you can also self-cater. Do try to combine a visit with the season of concerts of Baroque, classical and regional music at the Casa de Mateus, and perhaps the grape harvest too. Vila Real is just 20 minutes away, but you'll probably not even want to leave this place, which is perfect for meditation, fresh air and peace.

**Rooms:** 4 with bath & wc.
**Price:** Double/Twin Esc 13,000;
Apartment Esc 20,000.
**Breakfast:** Esc 1000.
**Meals:** Dinner Esc 2,500, available with notice.
**Closed:** Never.

From Vila Real take N332 past Mateus to S. Martinho de Anta; turn right onto N322-2 towards Gouvinhas. Immediately before Gouvinhas right for Guiães follow road past Quinta do Barreiro Baixo, follow signs to Barreiro (Alto) on unmade road.

Entry no: 24

Map no: 2

# Casa das Cardosas

Rua Central
Folhadela
5000 Vila Real
Trás-os-Montes

**Tel:** 259 331487
962 929750 (mob)
**Fax:** 259 331487

**Maria Teresa Cardosa Barata Lima**

What views! Although you are just a mile from Vila Real this grand Trás-os-Montes manor enjoys as bucolic a setting as you could hope to find; the hills roll out before you, sprinkled with white villages and farmsteads. The Cardosa family has been here for more than 250 years and once made wine here; the gardens produce peaches, plums, cherries and raspberries, and there's an attractive pool area. Find time to let the warm-natured Maria Teresa tell you a little of the area's history. Her three bedrooms are quiet, elegantly decorated and have not a hint of hotel. There are rugs and shining parquet, and one bedroom has a wonderfully ornate *Bilros* four-poster; the green room has a chandelier and pretty fabrics; and the smallest room has direct access to the terrace and its views. The lounge and dining room have parquet floors and period tables and chairs; cut flowers and family mementoes, displayed in glass wall cabinets, heighten the mood of unaffected intimacy. Breakfast at Cardosas is a generous meal with home-made jams, juices and eggs; at dinner you may be treated to roast beef or hake from the wood-fired oven. Make sure you have time to explore the Alvão Natural Park.

**Rooms:** 3 with bath or shower & wc.
**Price:** Double/Twin Esc 11,000; Single Esc 9,000.
**Breakfast:** Included.
**Meals:** Lunch/dinner on request, Esc 2,500.
**Closed:** Never.

In Vila Real go to University and here, to left of main entrance, house is signposted.

## Casa Agrícola da Levada
Timpeira
5000-419 Vila Real
Trás-os-Montes

**Tel:** 259 322190 / 323121
**Fax:** 259 346955
**E-mail:** levada@netc.pt

**Álbano Paganini da Costa Lobo**

In 1922, Levada stood alone, but the expansion of Vila Real has brought new neighbours and roads. Nevertheless it has kept its charm and there are long walks out from the house, quiet spots galore in the grounds and fishing in the River Corgo that cuts across the estate. House and chapel were the Portuguese answer to the French Art Deco. It is most attractive: granite offset by white rendering and burgundy windows and doors. There are four stonewalled guest rooms whose comfortable beds and utter quiet guarantee a deep sleep. In this house, the arts are celebrated, in paintings, sculptures and work by Álbano, a professional photographer. Young, friendly and gracious, Inês and Álbano always find time to share conversation – in the evening over wine or with coffee at breakfast. Food is especially good at Levada: home-made breads and jams (in the garden in summer) and dinners lovingly prepared. Nearly all is home-grown, home-produced or home-baked, and much of it is organic. There is a good house red or finer wines if you prefer. At nearby Casa Mateus there are concerts and music courses during the summer months. Álbano is involved and will tell you what's on.

**Rooms:** 4 with bath & wc;
1- and 2-bedroom suites.
**Price:** Double/Twin Esc 10,000-12,000,
Suite Esc 16,000-24,000.
**Breakfast:** Included.
**Meals:** On request Esc 2,500-3,500.
**Closed:** Never.

From Porto IP4 towards Bragança. Exit for Vila Real Norte then follow signs for centre; at BP station turn left towards Sabrosa. At junction (Palácio of Mateus to right) turn left, through Murça, over railway then river and house to right.

# Quinta do Real

Matosinhos
5400 Chaves
Trás-os-Montes

**Tel:** 276 966253
**Fax:** 276 965240

**Ramiro Guerra**

You would travel far to find as elegant a building or as wonderful a rural setting as the Quinta do Real. The façade is a masterpiece of understated elegance. Long and low, it looks somehow gentle – the feminine touch perhaps, for it was built in 1697 for the Vice Countess of Rio Maior. You pass through the entrance portal, which is topped by a granite cross, to enter a cobbled courtyard. We would choose a room in the main house with views across the valley, probably the master bedroom, but they all are large (except the attic room), spotlessly clean and prettily decorated with good-looking antiques. The other rooms are in outbuildings facing the patio; these are more basic but have more privacy. Back in the house is a cosy sitting room with a woodburning stove and another much larger one with a minstrels' gallery. The dining room is a delightful space, too; it has a chandelier, single table and a tallboy brimming with old china and glass. Your hosts are the charming Dona Celeste, who has lived there all her life, and her son Ramiro; he recently left a city career to dedicate himself to the house. There are a pool and barbecue outside, and horse-riding can be arranged.

**Rooms:** 10 with bath or shower & wc.
**Price:** Double 11,000-12,000; Twin Esc 12,000-13,000; Single Esc 10,000-11,000.
**Breakfast:** Included.
**Meals:** Packed lunch on request, Esc 3,500.
**Closed:** Never.

From Vidago towards Loivos, then right for Quinta do Real. Through forest to village of Matosinhos: through village, then follow signs to Quinta.

**Map no: 2**

# Quinta da Mata

Estrada de Valpaços
5400 Chaves
Trás-os-Montes

**Tel:** 276 340030
**Fax:** 276 340038
**E-mail:** quinta.mata@netc.pt

**Filinto Moura Morais**

Filinto found this 17th-century Trás-os-Montes house in ruins and completely
restored it, keeping nearly all the original features. He has made his ideals a reality
and is endearingly enthusiastic about his home and this region's people and their
food. For breakfast try miniature pasties, home-made bread, local Chaves ham and
perhaps some smoked sausage. For dinner he may suggest kid or a delicious *cozido*
(thick stew) and will certainly encourage you to try the wine from Valpaços.
Quinta da Mata's bedrooms are as special as your host. The craftsmanship of the
wooden floors and ceilings perfectly sets off the walls of dressed stone and hand-
painted tiles; Arraiolos rugs, crocheted bedcovers, repro beds and cut flowers lend
warmth to large spaces. You might choose the Presidential suite which has an
office/library, or the Imperial which is more private and has a whirlpool bath.
There are two tennis courts, a sauna, free use of bikes and walks through the
thickly wooded slopes of the Brunheiro mountains. "Filinto is charm itself," said
our inspector, who has marvellous memories of afternoon tea with him and a table
groaning under cheese, jam, doughnuts and cake.

**Rooms:** 6 with bath or shower & wc.
**Price:** Single Esc 10,000-12,000;
Double/Twin Esc 11,000-14,000.
**Breakfast:** Included.
**Meals:** Dinner Esc 2,000-3,000.
**Closed:** Never.

Just outside Chaves take N213 to Valpaços,
go through Nantes and the Quinta is well
signposted.

# Solar das Arcas

Arcas
5340-031 Macedo de Cavaleiros
Trás-os-Montes

**Tel:** 278 400010/401422
**Fax:** 278 401233

### Maria Francisca Pessanha Machado

In a forgotten, wine-growing corner of Portugal this lovely mansion has dignified the centre of the village of Arcas for over 300 years. The owners are direct descendants of Manuel Pessanha of Genoa, who came to teach the Portuguese the art of navigation. The house lies at the centre of a large estate of fruit orchards and olive groves. The pool is set in a walled courtyard. The main house is beautifully-proportioned; carved mouldings surround windows and doors while the family coat of arms above the portal reminds you that this is a noble house – as do the imposing private chapel, *sala de piano*, ancient panelled ceilings (one octagonal) and stone staircase. "Cosy privacy" is how the brochure (correctly) describes rooms and apartments (the latter in outbuildings). There are very comfy sofas and superb antique beds. Food? Forgive us for quoting the Arcas brochure again: "You will feel that you belong to a real Portuguese family when you sit on a footstool savouring a glass of wine and nibbling at a piece of a smoked delicacy before the fireplace where iron vessels boil and the revolving plate grills simple, but first-rate meals". And the *vinho* is included in the price.

**Rooms:** 1 suite, 3 one-bed and 2 two-bed apartments.
**Price:** Suite Esc 19,000; 1-bed Apartment (for 2) Esc 14,000; 2-bed Apartment (for 4) Esc 24,000. Add 5% VAT. Rates 20% higher in July/August.
**Breakfast:** Included.
**Meals:** Lunch/dinner on request, Esc 5,000-6,000.
**Closed:** Never.

From IP4 exit for Macedo de Cavaleiros. Here right onto N15 towards Zoio and after 1.7km left via Ferreira to Arcas. House in village centre.

**Map no: 2**

# Estalagem do Caçador

Largo Manuel Pinto de Azevedo  
5340 Macedo de Cavaleiros  
Trás-os-Montes

**Tel:** 278 426356/54  
**Fax:** 278 426381

### Maria Antonia Pinto de Azevedo

"Are you tired of big town's rush and longing for mountain's fresh air?" (sic) enquires the Estalagem's brochure. Well, perhaps you are and, providing you're not vehemently anti-hunting you should enjoy staying at this handsome hotel. Even our normally vegetarian inspector forgot the meat issue and awarded it a near-perfect score! Once the town hall of Macedo, it burnt down and the present owner's great-grandfather turned it into a hotel 40 years ago. His collection of prints and Toby jugs are still on display, but his first love was hunting: from your deeply comfortable armchair in bar and lounge you look up to antlers, shotguns and prints of horse and hounds; there are stuffed birds and leopard skins and photographs of huntsmen and their trophies. The bedrooms also have the hunt theme: prints and paintings of birds, pheasants, buffalo, rabbits together with *toile de Jouy* and some interesting antiques. Maria gives a warm welcome at this unusual hotel; it was she who crocheted the rabbits on your bedroom curtains. There is an excellent restaurant – locals come for the trout and ribs of wild boar. The journey takes you through dramatic scenery – an integral part of the experience.

**Rooms:** 25 with bath or shower & wc.  
**Price:** Single Esc 10,000-12,000;  
Double/Twin Esc 13,000-16,000.  
**Breakfast:** Included.  
**Meals:** Lunch/dinner Esc 3,000.  
**Closed:** December 24-25.

Turn off the Porto to Bragança road at Macedo do Cavaleiros, turn left in the centre of the town.

# Quinta do Conde

Gouvinhas                          **Tel:** 259 323 121
Sabrosa                            **Fax:** 259 326 553
5060 Vila Real                     **E-mail:** casamateus@telepac.pt
Trás-os-Montes

**Fernando Albuquerque**

This old stone house has character and quality. Housekeeper Lucia is kindness itself, very helpful, and proud of the house, which is spotlessly clean. The views over the hills and down the valley are stunning, and the house, set in a vineyard, has a good atmosphere thanks to Lucia's care and the architecture itself; exposed stone walls, slate floors and chestnut shutters, doors, wardrobes and panelling which are all well-made. The bedrooms are all different, not overly fussy, with comfortable beds and good views; three of the twin rooms have more modern bathrooms, and the quality throughout is good. The two sitting rooms are inviting. One has stone floors, rugs and sofas, the other slate floors, a sofa, card table and wood panel ceiling. The dining room is well proportioned and centres on a 10-seat round table with granite base. At the front of the house there are places to sit and enjoy the magnificent views of Trás-os-Montes ('across the mountains') – which you can also enjoy from the comfort of the pool. Ideal for those who want to get away from it all, not forgetting that the area has much of natural and historical interest.

**Rooms:** 7 with bath & wc.
**Price:** Esc 10,000.
**Breakfast:** Esc 1,000.
**Meals:** Dinner Esc 2,500.
**Closed:** Never.

From Vila Real take N322 past Casa de Mateus towards Sabrosa. At S. Martinho do Anta; right onto N322-2 direction Gouvinhas. After the town continue for 1.5km; house signed on right.

**Map no: 2**                                    Entry no: 31

# Quinta de la Rosa

5085 Pinhão
Douro

**Tel:** 254 732254 (UK 01296 748989)
**Fax:** 254 732346 (UK 01296 747212)
**E-mail:** sophia@quintadelarosa.com
**Web:** www.quintadelarosa.com

### Sophia Bergqvist

If you like port, then do stay as guests of the Bergqvists. The family have been in the trade for nearly 200 years and, as is usual in the industry, the estate matures its wines 'in house' and sells direct to customers. What better incentive to come? But first a hard choice is yours between a room or your very own Douro farmhouse. Three new bedrooms share a terrace high above the Douro whilst those in the main house are lower and nearer to the river. All are special; some have brightly-painted Alentejo furniture, others are more antique. *Dona Clara* has its own little lounge and a view of Pinhão. Of the two houses, each with its own pool, we loved *Lamelas*, hidden away at the very top of the estate and approached through a forest. It is splendidly decorated and equipped with space enough for a large family or group. *Amerela* (in the large photo), further down the hill, has similar standards of décor. If you're not into self-catering breakfast in the light, sunny dining room with more of that view, housekeeper Filomena will help. First priority must be a tour of the cellars and a port tasting followed, perhaps, by a cruise on the river. In September, join in with the grape harvest.

**Rooms:** 5 rooms & 1 suite; 2 self-catering houses.
**Price:** Double/Twin Esc 12,500; Suite Esc 16,500. Houses (for 6-8) £315-£830.
**Breakfast:** Included.
**Meals:** None available.
**Closed:** Never.

From Regna cross bridge, driving up river. Just before Pinhão, Quinta de la Rosa visible on the other side, drive through village and back along to La Quinta.

# Casa de Casal de Loivos

Casal de Loivos          **Tel:** 254 732149
5085-010 Pinhão          **Fax:** 254 732149
Douro                    **E-mail:** casadecasaldeloivos@ip.pt

**Manuel Bernardo de Sampayo**

One of the best views in this book – and anywhere! Built in 1658, this northern manor has been home to the Sampayos since 1733. The house is in the village, yet so placed that from the front you see no other dwelling, only the River Douro far below, slowly winding its way through steep hills terraced with vineyards. It is a marvellous sight; every room opens to it. Tradition, comfort and gentility are the hallmarks here. Manuel is a truly old-fashioned, charming gentleman; he speaks perfect English and usually sports a cravat – it's certainly a place where you dress for dinner. Traditional meat and fish dishes are created from old family recipes, and are always excellent. The dining room is simply beautiful, dominated by the large communal table – Manuel calls it "English-inn style". There is a comfortable sitting room which opens onto the terrace, below which is the pool and another terrace. The view-filled bedrooms are gorgeous, elegantly furnished and have good bathrooms. Fortified by good food and wine, well cared for by Manuel and his staff of nine, and able to watch the interplay of light, land and water for miles and miles, you'll feel somewhere halfway between earth and heaven.

**Rooms:** 6 with bath & wc.
**Price:** Double/Twin Esc 16,000; Single Esc 13,000.
**Breakfast:** Included.
**Meals:** Dinner Esc 4,500, by arrangement.
**Closed:** Christmas & January.

From Pinhão take road to Alijó; take the first right and go up and up through vinyards until village of Casal de Loivos. House on right at the end of the village.

**Map no: 2**                    Entry no: 33

# Casa de Visconde de Chanceleiros

Largo da Fonte
Chanceleiros – Covas do Douro
5085-202 Pinhão
Douro

**Tel:** 254 730190
**Fax:** 254 730199
**Web:** www.chanceleiros.co.uk

### Kurt & Ursula Böcking

This house has everything in abundance: big comfortable beds, squashy armchairs, lovely bathrooms, thick fluffy towels, great views, lots of space inside and out, and friendly hosts and dogs. Kurt and Ursula's home is a classic granite and white manor house on the edge of a hillside village, with terraces on one side. Wide granite steps lead down to the terrace where there is a large swimming pool with a long roofed *cabana*, inside which you'll find a sofa, stereo and tables. The house is tasteful and stylish, informal without being too casual. The hosts are very welcoming, and so, too, is housekeeper Adelaide; she has been there 30 years. "We live with our guests, that's the difference," says Ursula. Inside, there are lots of warm colours and in the large bedrooms, which have colour themes, you'll find beautifully hand-painted furniture and beds. These rooms are rather like big bed-sitting rooms, and one is on two floors, ideal for a family. In the common rooms Ursula has created combinations of warm colours and fabrics, the furniture a mixture of antiques and modern pieces. Breakfasts are feasts, and don't miss the splendid dinners. To follow, there's ping-pong, pool, squash, *boules* and jacuzzi.

**Rooms:** 6 with bath & wc.
**Price:** Double/Twin Esc 18,000-20,000; Single Esc 16,000-17,000; extra bed Esc 5,000.
**Breakfast:** Included.
**Meals:** Lunch Esc 3,000; 3-course dinner, Esc 4,500, on request.
**Closed:** Never.

From Pinhão, Chanceleiros is well signposed and house is on left when you get there.

# Casa da Levada

Travanca do Monte, Cx. 715
Bustelo
4600 Amarante
Douro

**Tel:** 255 43 38 33 M: 93 647 2946
**Fax:** 22 618 1516

**Maria Machado Teixeira de Vasconcelos do Cabo Cerqueira**

The great crenelated tower is visible as you come down the winding cobbled track into this ancient hilltop village, perched amid mountain views. Levada is really a small castle in a settlement built of rough-hewn, moss-covered granite blocks where people and animals still live cheek by jowl. Rough wooden doors open to reveal a goat, a pair of oxen, an old woman embroidering: scenes from centuries past. The house is a mountain refuge, and hosts Maria and Luís are wonderfully welcoming. She is an English teacher, he a humorous man whose family have lived here for 300 years. You'll sleep in bedrooms with granite walls, wooden ceilings, beams and sisal matting. The Tower bedroom has a separate bathroom across the landing, with low beams and a terracotta floor. Very unusual, the 'Poet's room' (*quarto do poeta*) has a trapdoor down to a bathroom. The lounge is comfortable and the dining room barn-like, with a large oval table at which everyone has breakfast (cooked by Luís) or dinner together; food is traditional and the wine comes from Luís's mother's farm. Up the hill, you pass granite water mills, and further up is a bleak hilltop with great boulders and dolmens. A marvellous place.

**Rooms:** 4 with bath & wc.
**Price:** Double/Twin Esc 12,000; Single Esc 9,600; Extra bed Esc 3,500.
**Breakfast:** Included.
**Meals:** Light meal Esc 2,000; dinner Esc 3,500.
**Closed:** Never.

From Amarante go towards Regua on N101 to Cavalinho; then after 6km turn right at sign for Casa de Levada.

Map no: 1

Entry no: 35

# Casa de Vilarinho de São Romão

Vilarinho de São Romão          **Tel:** 259 930754
5060 Sobrosa                    **Fax:** 259 930754
Douro                           **E-mail:** vilarinho@pax.jazznet.pt

**Cristina van Zeller**

This is a beautiful combination of old and new, of warm, sunny colours, light and space; the fruit of an excellent refurbishment of a 17th-century house overlooking the Pinhão valley (with a 1462 chapel at the entrance). Cristina's ancestors came to Portugal from Holland in the 18th century, and are an established port-wine family. She gave up teaching art to concentrate on the house, then a ruin, and then on the vineyards around it. The mood is light and airy, with pale wooden floors strewn with kilims and rugs, clear white walls, enormous rooms, grand paintings and fine antique furniture. The lounge is huge and comfortable, with large yellow sofas and lots of wood. Breakfast is generous, including fresh juice and fruit from the farm. The bedrooms continue the mood of the rest of the house. One has twin brass beds, rugs and a stone window seat, another a *Dona Maria* bed. Somehow, the long curtains and drapes and the natural materials go well together. Outside there is a shaded terrace, an inner gravelled courtyard with a pond, and plenty of walks around the vineyards and fruit trees and, always, those views across the Pinhão valley.

**Rooms:** 6 with bath & wc.
**Price:** Double/Twin Esc 15,000; Single Esc 12,000.
**Breakfast:** Included.
**Meals:** Dinner Esc 3,000, by arrangement.
**Closed:** Christmas.

From Vila Real to Pinhão through Sabrosa and when in village of Vilarinho de São Romão, you will see granite gateway and chapel on the left. Go through the gate.

# Casa dos Varais

5100-426 Lamego
Douro

**Tel:** 254 313251
**Fax:** 254 313251
**E-mail:** casadosvarais@clix.pt

**João Girão de Azeredo**

Overooking the Douro Valley and its terraces of vines, the Casa dos Varais is a large pink house whose patchy limewash lends an air of faded grandeur. It has a grand past, linked with many of Portugal's noble families. Today it appears on the labels of the estate's wines – well worth trying at dinner. João, who tends the vines, and his wife Mafalda, have four children and are very friendly; if you are interested João will show you around the *adega* and explain viniculture. The house has a rich, rather Edwardian atmosphere. The dining room and sitting room, and one of the bedrooms, have huge windows overlooking the river and Régua. The bedrooms belong to another age, with mahogany beds and marble wash basins – our favourite was the *passarinhos*, with its bird wallpaper. The bathroom, with its little bath and ducks on the tiles, is up a little flight of stairs. In the elegant dining room, with its long, lacy curtains and wooden Aboboda ceiling, pictures of the British Royals add to the regal mood. The separate, self-catering *Casa de Pinguéis* is well-equipped and has a similar atmosphere with rich Alcobaça fabrics and lots of exposed stone.

**Rooms:** 3 with bath & wc in house; self-catering house with 3 bedrooms.
**Price:** Double/Twin Esc 14,000; Single Esc 11,600; House Esc 35,000.
**Breakfast:** Incuded; house self-catering.
**Meals:** Dinner Esc 3,500, by arrangement.
**Closed:** B&B October 31-April 1; self-catering open all year.

From Régua cross the river towards Lamego, but turn immediately right towards Resende; the house is on the left, large and pink.

**Map no:** 1

Entry no: 37

# Casal de Aboadela

Aboadela
4600-500 Amarante
Douro

**Tel:** 255 441141 or
22 9513055

**José Silva Rebelo & family**

You'll long remember arriving at this old granite farm house; once you turn off the main road you twist and turn along the narrowest of lanes which leads you to this delightfully sleepy hamlet and old Douro farmhouse. There is many a treat in the rambling gardens: an old granite maize store, a bubbling spring, gourds and pumpkins drying in the sun. Old millstones recall the building's infancy. There are roses and oranges and vines and, in among them, secluded places for contemplation; it would be a perfect place to paint or read, such is the peace. Bedrooms and suite are in the main house, simply attired in cottage style with family furniture and lacking nothing; and just to one side in a converted outbuilding is the 'stone little house' (sic) which is self contained and would be just right for a longer stay. The guest sitting/dining room is similarly unpretentious: granite-walled with a tiled floor and potted plants. Home-grown wine is available. A French window gives onto a small balcony and lets in the morning light and the view. There are lovely rambles straight out from the house and the São Gonçalo monastery in Amarante is just a short drive away.

**Rooms:** 3 with bath & wc; 1 suite and 1 house.
**Price:** Double/Twin Esc 8,000-10,000; Suite Esc 10,000-16,000; house Esc 60,000 per week.
**Breakfast:** Included.
**Meals:** Picnics on request. Self-catering Little House has a barbecue.
**Closed:** Never.

From Amarante towards Vila Real on IP4.
9km after passing Amarante, right to Aboadela and follow signs for 'turismo rural', then 'tr' to the house.

# Casa d'Além
Oliveira
5040- 204 Mesão Frio
Douro

**Tel:** 254 321991
**Fax:** 254 321991

**Paulo Dias Pinheiro**

The cheerful façade of Casa d'Além looks out across the terraced vineyards of the Douro valley and reflects the optimism of the early '20s. It also suggests a rather diminutive residence, but behind its frontage the house widens out and becomes surprisingly large and airy, with far more than first impressions would suggest. The public rooms are the most refined: the Rennie Macintosh print on easy chairs, sofas and drapes is perfectly balanced by the delicate wrought-iron work of the balconies. Shining parquet, piano and card table create an atmosphere of old Portugal. Next door is a panelled dining room and, still more remarkable, a long painted corridor, a 'marbled sunburst', which leads to your bedroom. A feast of period pieces, there are rugs and marble-topped dressers, generous old tubs and wash stands. There are heavenly views from some rooms like *o quarto do Avó* and *o quarto azul*. Paulo and his wife speak excellent English and their marvellous housekeeper Maria will take care of you. Outside are views, pure air and a pleasing pool area. Inside, be sure not to miss dinner: perhaps a roast from their bread oven, home-made ice-cream and a chilled glass of the local wine.

**Rooms:** 4 with bath or shower & wc.
**Price:** Double/Twin Esc 13,000; Single Esc 10,000.
**Breakfast:** Included.
**Meals:** Lunch by arrangement; dinner Esc 3,500.
**Closed:** Never.

From Porto IP4 towards Vila Real, then N101 towards Mesão Frio. Here N108 towards Peso da Régua to Granjão. Under railway bridge then left to Oliveira and follow signs to Casa d'Além.

**Map no: 1**

# Casa das Torres de Oliveira

Oliveira
Vila Real
5040 Mesão Frio
Douro

**Tel:** 254 336743 or 21 840 6486
**Fax:** 254 336195 or 21 846 3319

### Isidora Reguela Benito Sousa Girão

Arriving in Oliveira, you won't miss this magnificent twin-towered building sitting proudly up on a hillside to one side of the village. This is a classic manor house, grand but welcoming. The estate's vineyards surround the house, and the grapes are for port as well as white and red Sedinhas, named after the present owner's seventh-removed grandfather who built the house. Cross a cobbled patio with a fountain to reach the main entrance; from here there are long views out across the valley and down to the river Douro which serpentines into the far distance. To one side of a high entrance hall, Oliveira's lounge is generous with space and light; it has a rugged parquet floor and sashed-back curtains to let in the glorious setting. Cushioned sofas, old china, a piano and a Madonna and Child speak of *velho Portugal*. From the high-ceilinged dining room, where there's port going back to 1888, you look out at the *adega* where vats of the estate's wine are stored; a bottle will be yours at dinner. Your bedroom will have a beautiful bed and dresser, rugs and lamps and a shining wooden floor; the tower room is a great favourite and well worth the price.

**Rooms:** 6 with bath & wc.
**Price:** Double/Twin Esc 18,500-20,000; Suite Esc 18,500-20,000; Single Esc 14,600-15,500; extra bed Esc 3,800-4,000.
**Breakfast:** Included.
**Meals:** Lunch, Esc 2,000; dinner Esc 3,500.
**Closed:** November-March.

From Porto IP4 towards Vila Real to Amarante. Here take N101 towards Mesão Frio, then N108 towards Régua. In village of Granjão turn left to Olivera (just before bridge and signs Qtas du Douro). After 3km second left to Oliveira: house on right.

# Quinta da Granja

Rua Manuel Francisco de Araujo, 444    **Tel:** 229 710147
Aguas Santas-Maia                       96 2769206 (mob)
4445-120 Ermesinde/Águas Santas
Douro

### António Nunes da Ponte

Porto and its hectic pace may be close at hand but behind its high stone walls the Quinta da Granja's setting is very rural. This genteel *solar* dates from the 18th century, though parts of the estate are older. The gardens, with their ancient stands of camellias, azaleas and carefully trimmed box, were planted some 400 years ago. Both house and gardens (the latter now overlooked by younger tower blocks) have been sensitively restored by António Nunes da Ponte. Things are on a grand scale here, and the lounge is more than 100 feet long; it still feels most welcoming with its terracotta floor, rugs, period furnishing, wall hangings and family portraits in oil and photo. At one end it leads through into the solar's gilded Baroque chapel – nowadays only used for family weddings and other special occasions. The bedrooms have a mood of simple elegance; there are handsome *Dona Maria* beds, high-quality drapes, carpeted floors and period bedside tables. Stay a couple of days and find a favourite spot in the garden, an oasis in the urban landscape which surrounds it; come late winter or early spring to see the camellias at their very best.

**Rooms:** 3 with bath & wc.
**Price:** Single Esc 15,500; Double/Twin Esc 20,000.
**Breakfast:** Included.
**Meals:** None available.
**Closed:** November 1-April 30.

From Porto towards Braga/Vila Real on ring road, then A4 towards Vila Real. Take first exit for Ermesinde/Rio Tinto, then left towards Alto da Maia. After 500m over bridge then immediately left and first right. Watch for small 'turismo' sign.

## Pensão Estoril
Rua de Cedofeita, 193
4050-179 Porto
Douro

**Tel:** 22 200 2751 / 5152
**Fax:** 22 2082468
**E-mail:** estoril@usa.net

**Benvinda & Joaquim Santos**

We include this little family-run boarding house because it is central, clean and a good base if your purse doesn't stretch to the rather grander hotels of Porto. Rua de Cedofeita is one of the city's liveliest (pedestrianised) shopping streets. Halfway along, Pensão Estoril occupies a 1900s town house. The pension – reached by the original bannistered staircase winding its elegant way up to the top floor – has been in the care of Benvinda and Joaquim for 25 years. Kinder folk you could not hope to meet. Bedrooms are simple, some of them curiously shaped around the bath and shower rooms which were added piecemeal over the years. We'd prefer one of those looking out over the garden at the back, a rare expanse of green in this part of the city. Most have small shower rooms, are carpeted and have phones, and the upstairs ones are surprisingly quiet. The terrace to the rear looks out across the garden, a place to unwind after a day of visits in this fascinating city. A reliable and inexpensive alternative with good food downstairs and plenty of places to eat close by.

**Rooms:** 14 with bath & wc, 3 with shower & wc.
**Price:** Single Esc 4,000-5,500; Double/Twin Esc 5,500-7,400; 3 person Esc 6,800-9,600; 4 person Esc 8,400-10,600.
**Breakfast:** Included.
**Meals:** None available.
**Closed:** Never.

Arriving in Porto, follow signs into cente; head for 'Palácio de Cristal/Torre dos Clérigos', then to 'Praça Coronel Pacheco' (ask). Leave car in parking 'Praça Coronel Pacheco' in front of police station. Estoril 100m.

# Casa do Marechal

Avenida do Boavista 2674
4100-119 Porto
Douro

**Tel:** 22 610 4702 / 03 /04/ 05
**Fax:** 22 610 3241
**E-mail:** casa.marechal@mail.telepac.pt

**João Paulo Baganha**

Elegant, cream and white, utterly-deco Casa do Marechal was built in 1940 and would sit as happily on the front in Miami as it does here in one of Porto's smarter residential areas. It looks like a wedding cake, with a rich layer of cream stucco running round at second floor level. Inside, things are just as flamboyant; the present owners have transformed an already grand house into a refined and luxurious guesthouse. There are just five bedrooms, decked out in pink, blue, green, beige and yellow. They are good-sized and carefully manicured; beds are five-star, each has a small writing table and all the usual modern extras, even hydro-massage tubs with sparkling tiles all round. There is an orange-coloured lounge with a balcony, a roof terrace and a garden with shady corners. At breakfast you can expect all the normal things plus fresh fruit and even porridge. The restaurant serves dinners on weekdays; everything's bought fresh at the local market. The owners describe the food as "a new gastronomic interpretation of French and Portuguese traditional cuisine", and vegetarian food can be prepared. (You may need the gym, sauna and Turkish bath in the basement!)

**Rooms:** 5 with bath & wc.
**Price:** Double/Twin Esc 25,000-28,000.
**Breakfast:** Included.
**Meals:** Lunch/Dinner Esc 6,000.
Restaurant closed at weekends.
**Closed:** August & Christmas.

Arriving on motorway from Lisbon after toll booths towards Arrabida, then Boa Vista and then Foz/Castelo do Queijo. Hotel on right after 3km. The hotel has its own parking.

**Map no: 1**

## Residencial Castelo Santa Catarina

Rua Santa Catarina 1347
4000-457 Porto
Douro

**Tel:** 22 509 5599
**Fax:** 22 550 6613

João Brás

This eye-catching building was built high up above Porto during the period which the Portuguese call the Gothic Revival. Even if the corner turrets and window arches don't remind you of Notre Dame, you can't fail to be intrigued by this tile-clad edifice, which stands like a folly, surrounded by swaying palms, in an otherwise rather conservative suburb of the city. The interior décor is as extravagant as the building's exterior. You are regaled by gilt and stucco, chandeliers and mirrors, cherubs and lozenges, Tiffany lamps and roses, repro beds and cavernous wardrobes. It is showy, over the top, faded in parts, rather garish in others and incredible fun. Your choice of carpet colour? Turquoise, lime green or perhaps a navy paisley print. There is the odd patch of peeling paint, the bathroom tiles are often out of step with the rooms but the whiff of the past is a part of the charm of the place. The owner's affable son João is normally about in reception and with fluent English can answer all your questions about this whimsical building. Try and book the Tower suite; it's worth the extra for the views. An enormously entertaining city hotel.

**Rooms:** 21 with bath or shower & wc; 3 suites.
**Price:** Single Esc 7,500; Double/Twin Esc 11,000; Suite Esc 15,000.
**Breakfast:** Included.
**Meals:** None available.
**Closed:** Never.

At the top of Rua Santa Catarina, just below Plaza Marques Pombal, follow signs and ask directions!

Beira
•
Estremadura
•
Ribatejo

# Central Portugal

"I am very happy here, because I loves oranges, and talks bad Latin to the monks... and I swims in the Tagus all across at once, and I ride on an ass or a mule, and swears Portuguese, and have... bites from the mosquitos. But what of that? Comfort must not be expected by folks that go a-pleasuring?"     Lord Byron

# Casa das Ribas

Castelo
4520 Santa Maria da Feira
Beira

**Tel:** 256 373485 / 21 797 1984
**Fax:** 256 37 34 85

**Maria Carmina Vaz de Oliveira**

Opposite a castle in woods above the town, you walk into the enormous entrance hall and another age. Over a double pony-cart hangs a large family coat of arms; this is a stately home with chandeliers and beautiful furnishings everywhere. Nonetheless, its atmosphere is easy and lived in and Maria Carmina and her family enjoy having guests and speaking English with them. The bedrooms are traditional and luxurious with a selection of Dom José and Edwardian beds and have modern bathrooms. The suite is more modern and very attractive, with seven windows overlooking the gardens. The separate, rustic Casa do Caseiro has a huge double bedroom and is, said our inspector, "the most gorgeous holiday cottage". In the main house you breakfast in the old kitchen near its vast fireplace. You can relax in several drawing rooms, in the *Sala da Musica*, with its grand piano, grand sofa and fireplace, and explore the beautiful dining room, which opens onto the gardens. Maria has green fingers and this place is a must if you love gardens; parts are park-like, with hydrangeas, rhododendrons, roses, palms and cedars. Do explore the library, the games room and the beautiful 16th-century chapel.

**Rooms:** 5 with bath & wc; 1 suite and 1 2-bedroom separate house.
**Price:** Double/Twin Esc 12,000-14,000; Single Esc 8,000-10,000; Suite Esc 14,000-15,000; House Esc 15,000 per night, Esc 70,000 per week.
**Breakfast:** Included.
**Meals:** None; self-catering in house.
**Closed:** Never.

Come off Lisboa/Porto motorway at Feira and follow signs for Castelo; you can see the castle in trees on way into Feira; the house is next to castle.

Entry no: 45

Map no: 1

# Casa Campo das Bizarras

Rua da Capela 76
Fareja
3600-271 Castro Daire
Beira

**Tel:** 232 386 107
**Fax:** 232 382 044

**Marina Moutinho**

First impressions are deceptive, because from the road you first see the back of the house, but as you enter the garden a lovely old granite farmhouse is revealed. The garden and orchard are a sheer delight, the joint passions of Marina, a retired science teacher. She is an excellent hostess, and clearly loves what was her grandfather's house. It has bags of genuine rustic character, with walls of great blocks of stone, assorted tile and wood floors, wooden beams and ceilings. Some bedrooms are in the main house including a slipper double, but most are in outbuildings. Some have kitchenettes hidden in furniture, so the country character is maintained and you can still make your own meals – or buy a fresh trout and grill it on the terrace barbecue. The rooms are small and full of old domestic and rural-abilia. The lounge is upstairs and has a leather sofa, fireplace, big beams and ceramics on display; the reading room is downstairs, where there's also a bar and pool table. It's very cosy, easy to get used to, and there are lots of places to sit and relax, inside and out.

**Rooms:** 7 with bath & shower & wc;
4 apartments.
**Price:** Double/Twin Esc 10,500-12,000;
Single Esc 8,500-9,500; Apartment for 2
(per week) Esc 87,000-94,000; Apartment
(for 4) Esc 129,000-136,000.
**Breakfast:** Included.
**Meals:** Dinner Esc 3,000, by arrangement.
**Closed:** November 1- March.

From Castro Daire follow road sign to Fareginha. When at Fareja turn left at sign for Turismo Rural. Past church, up narrow cobbled lane, Bizarras is on the right.

**Map no: 1**

**Entry no: 46**

# Quinta da Timpeira

Lugar de Timpeira
5100-718 Lamego
Beira

**Tel:** 254 612811
**Fax:** 254 615176
**E-mail:** quintadatimpeira@portugalmail.pt

**Francisco Parente**

A modern-looking home close to the Sanctuary of Nossa Senhora dos Remédios, an important pilgrimage site; many climb the the 700 steps on their knees, and countless miracles are attributed to Our Lady. You will be well looked after here by Francisco, an optometrist, and Isabel, a civil engineer. The house is bordered by a crisp, topiaried box hedge and below are terraces with pool, tennis court, fruit trees and four hectares of vines; opposite are the Meadas mountains and behind are vineyards which supply the nearby Raposeira sparkling wine factory. The house is unfussy and, while the bedrooms are not particularly large, they are neatly decorated with good quality furniture and wooden or iron beds. Floors are wooden with rugs and bathrooms convey a smartness despite their grey tiles. The sitting/dining room is modern and unusual with a long curved wall – there are great views from its enormous window and balcony. Here you can have a traditional Portuguese dinner with Timpeira and other wines included. There's a small 'shop' downstairs where you can buy local handicrafts and you'll find a games room, bar and wine cellar, too.

**Rooms:** 7 with bath or shower & wc.
**Price:** Double/Twin Esc 12,000; Single Esc 9,500.
**Breakfast:** Included.
**Meals:** Lunch/dinner by arrangement Esc 3,500.
**Closed:** Never.

From Lamego take the N2. The Quinta is 2.5km after the Raposeird sparkling wine factory, on the left.

# Casa da Mota

Lugar da Mota
Carvalhais
3660 São Pedro do Sul
Beira

**Tel:** 232 798202/ 21 726 2315/
91 766 3739 (mob)
**Web:** www.turism.net/casadamota

**Maria Eugénia Raposo**

At the foot of the Serra da Arade mountains, this house has been in the Raposo family since it was built in the 18th century. You enter through large gates and then cross a granite bridge to the first floor. The floors and walls are made from giant blocks of granite, most of them left as plain stone. In the bedrooms one wall has been left bare, the others plastered. They have wooden ceilings and floors, antique beds, and excellent bathrooms. In a separate house, which can be self-catering, there are metal and chestnut four-posters; all the bedclothes and pillowcases display the family crest. The main house has a big party room and a cosy sitting room. There is a venerable grandfather clock, and the old bread oven hides a TV. Breakfast is generous and includes juice from the orange trees next to the house; you can eat out on the terrace, or enjoy the views from the pool. There is a big kitchen in the separate house and a kitchenette in the main house, so you can make your own meals. (There is a very good restaurant a five-minute walk away.) Maria Eugénia will tell you about local places of interest; there is marvellous walking, and the area has springs, horse-riding and history.

**Rooms:** 6 with bath & wc and 1 separate house.
**Price:** Double/Twin Esc 13,000; Apartment Esc 20,000.
**Breakfast:** Included.
**Meals:** None; self-catering possible.
**Closed:** Never.

From the IP5 Aveiro/Vizeu go to S. Pedro do Sul. In town turn right at signposts for S. Cruz da Tropa; after 4km turn right for Fraguinha; after 500m follow signs for Casa da Mota for 1km, through pine forest, then village. House is on the left.

**Map no: 1**

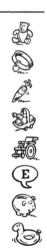

# Quinta da Comenda

3660 São Pedro do Sul      **Tel:** 232 711101 or 22 6183491
Beira      **Fax:** 232 711101 or 22 6183491
     **E-mail:** quintacomenda@hotmail.com

**Maria Laura Cardoso da Rocha**

This lovely group of buildings is softened by a rampant camellia which lends swathes of colour when in flower. Lovers of organic wine may have heard of Quinta da Comenda; it exports its prize-winning whites and rosés all over the world. What you probably won't have heard is that the first King of Portugal, Dom Afonso Enriques, did battle nearby, broke a leg and was forced to stay at his uncle's place, the Quinta da Comenda. It later passed into the hands of the Order of Malta, hence the cross above the main entrance. Guest rooms match expectations after such an impressive arrival: polished parquet floors, elegant antique beds and pretty tiles in the bathroom. Lounge and dining room double up in a huge *salão* which leads to the old wine cellar, and you are treated to a real feast at the breakfast table. Little details such as the fruit basket and bottled water in your room show how much the Rocha family care. Wander down to the river and a Roman bridge, through the vineyards and orchards, stock up on wine and find time to chat with your charming hosts. On most Saturdays in summer there are wedding parties; the ivy-clad chapel is to one end of the courtyard.

**Rooms:** 6 with bath or shower & wc; 1 apartment for 4 with kitchenette.
**Price:** Single Esc 8,800-11,600; Double/Twin Esc 10,700-14,000; Apartment (for 4) Esc 22,400.
**Breakfast:** Included.
**Meals:** None available.
**Closed:** Never.

From Viseu IP5 towards S. Pedro do Sul on N16. A few km before S. Pedro follow 'Agro Turismo' sign; Quinta on left, well signposted.

# Casa de Sol Nascente

Taipa
3800-981 Aveiro
Beira

**Tel:** 234 933597
**Fax:** 234 933598
**E-mail:** np21cc@mail.telepac.pt
**Web:** www.aveiro.co.pt/solnascente

**Ian M Arbuckle**

East meets west in 'the house of the rising sun'. The architecture is the work of Ian's Japanese wife Chizu, an original artist whose beautifully exotic paintings hang in many rooms (and in the Tokyo National Gallery, too). You enter to see a column of glass around which curves a flight of stairs; there is light everywhere thanks to the large windows. Some walls are curved, too, which casts graduated shadows. Chizu is fond of the roundness of the place: "Curves bring nature into the living room and soften the mood," she says. The rooms contain a successful blend of pieces from around the world; the two suites, Acacia and Bamboo, are beautifully furnished. Chizu and Ian are easy and well travelled (he worked in many parts of the world before settling here). They are excellent hosts and effortlessly create a gentle mood and a family atmosphere – this is a great place to come with your children. Meals are superb and span a wide range of Portuguese and Japanese cooking; in the summer they do excellent barbecues. Nearby are the famous Aveiro lagoons, full of wildlife, and the sea is 10km away.

**Rooms:** 2 with bath & wc; 2 suites.
**Price:** Double/Twin Esc 8900; Suite Esc 15,600; Apartment (for 6) Esc 186,000 per week.
**Breakfast:** Included.
**Meals:** Lunch/dinner on request, Esc 5,000; snacks Esc 1,500.
**Closed:** Never.

*Map will be sent to guests.* From the A1 turn off at the Aveiro Sul, Águeda exit; after toll gate turn right onto EN235, towards Aveiro; after 500m, right to Mamodeiro, at the first café, first right again to Requeixo. Follow road until Taipa. Take road as it bends down to the right; at the bend take smaller road going up on your right; follow to the last house, 800m.

**Map no: 1**

# Solar do Ervedal

Rua Dr. Francisco Brandão 12
3408-063 Ervedal da Beira
Beira

**Tel:** 238 644283
**Fax:** 238 641133
**E-mail:** solardoervedal@mail.telepac.pt

### Maria Helena de Albuquerque

Though architectural styles have come and gone, this noble 500-year-old
residence, built in granite, has never left the hands of the descendants of Diogo
Braz Pinto. High walls surround the estate; you enter through elegant wrought-
iron gates and once within it seems hard to imagine you are still in the village. A
cobbled courtyard replete with pots of geraniums fronts the house; behind it are
acres of organically farmed orchards and a stand of 200-year-old oaks. Guest
rooms are in the south wing, the oldest part of the manor. The house is grand; the
large sitting room has an unusual octagonal ceiling, Gothic door arches of local
granite and two burgundy sofas pulled up to the hearth. It's good to see a
chessboard on display while the TV is hidden in a specially designed cupboard.
The dining room is just as delightful and eating in is recommended: roast duck
with rice is a speciality, desserts are delicious and wines are local. Bedrooms are
grand, centred on ornate beds and other fine antique furniture, and set off by
parquet floors, stuccoed ceilings and window seats. The present Viscountess Maria
Helena is a kind, gracious hostess and you will be reluctant to leave her superb
home.

**Rooms:** 5 with bath & wc; 1 suite.
**Price:** Single Esc 14,900; Double/Twin
Esc 17,000; Suite Esc 23,400.
**Breakfast:** Included.
**Meals:** Lunch/dinner on request,
Esc 3,500.
**Closed:** November & Christmas.

Just before the town centre of Oliveira do
Hospital (off N17 Coimbra – Guarda),
turn right just after VW garage to Ervedal
da Beira. 16km to village. The Solar is signposted from village centre.

**Map no: 1**

# Estalagem Casa D'Azurara

Rua Nova 78
3530 Mangualde
Beira

**Tel:** 232 612010
**Fax:** 232 622575
**E-mail:** casa.azurara@esoterica.pt
**Web:** www.casa-azurara.pt

**Aldina Salgado**

In a quiet corner of a sleepy town Casa D'Azurara is a perfect place to unwind and let yourself be pampered. This manor house was built by the Counts of Mangualde in the 17th century, added to at the end of the 19th century and renovated to create a small, luxurious hotel. There are two guest sitting rooms downstairs; one has an enormous old granite hearth, the other high French windows with draped and flounced curtains. There are framed etchings, potted palms, books, cut flowers and a good choice of fabric on chairs and sofas. Carpeted corridors (a lift if you need it) lead to the rooms, where furnishing is either antique or repro; rich fabrics are used for bedspreads and curtains. Our choice would be suite-like 206; it has a sloping ceiling, *Dona Maria* beds and double French windows. Breakfast includes a choice of breads, cheeses and cold meats whilst the dinner menu has a strong regional bias; there are interesting fish dishes and a speciality is duck. Don't miss the gardens – magnolia, hortensias and camellia are all of an amazing size. The staff are caring and can organise wine tastings at nearby *adegas*. A place that successfully welcomes both business people and travellers.

**Rooms:** 14 with bath & wc & 1 suite.
**Price:** 'Superior' Double/Twin Esc 22,000;
Single Esc 20,500; 'Standard' Double/Twin
Esc 19,500; Single Esc 18,000; Suite Esc 26,000.
**Breakfast:** Included.
**Meals:** Lunch Esc 3,000; dinner
Esc 4,000.
**Closed:** Never.

From Porto IP5 towards Guarda. Exit for Mangualde;
Estalagem in town centre, signposted. Careful not to
confuse with 2nd modern Estalagem as you enter town.

**Map no: 1**

# Quinta da Ponte

Faia
6300 Guarda
Beira

**Tel:** 271 926126
**Fax:** 271 926126

**Maria Joaquina Aragão de Sousa Alvim**

Just a short drive from Guarda, at the edge of the Serra da Estrêla and beside an old Roman bridge that crosses the river Mondego, this elegant 17th-century manor house is as seductive as they come. The main façade is what first holds the eye; at one end is the Quinta's private chapel and next to it a granite portal leads through to the inner courtyard. The dining room is in what was once the stable block; the granite feeding troughs have been kept as a feature but you will eat your (generous) breakfast from a china plate. Choose between a room in the old house or a modern apartment looking across the pool to the park beyond. Rooms are light (French windows on two sides), decorated in greens and pinks, tiled throughout and each has a sitting room with hearth; furniture is a mix of old and new, but the feeling throughout is of unfolding history. There is a second, larger guest sitting room in a modern building next to the apartments. The bedrooms maintain the period feeling with lovely carved wooden beds. Do explore the walks along the river and the beautiful and well-designed garden that combines the natural and the neatly-clipped.

**Rooms:** 2 with bath & wc; 5 apartments.
**Price:** Twin Esc 17,000; Apartment (for 2) Esc 18,500; Single Esc 14,500.
**Breakfast:** Included.
**Meals:** None available.
**Closed:** October-Easter, except New Year & Carnival.

Coming from Lisbon leave the IP5 at exit 26 for the EN16 towards Porto da Carne. House signposted to right; follow road down to river and house (signposted 'Turismo de Habitação').

Entry no: 53

Map no: 2

# Casa das Tílias

São Romão
6270-257 Seia
Beira

**Tel:** 238 390055
**Fax:** 238 390123
**E-mail:** casa.tilias@mail.telepac.pt
**Web:** www.tilias.com

### José L. Figueiredo Lopes

This is an ideal place if you want to combine the rigours of mountain walks (you are at the heart of the Serra da Estrêla Nature Park) with the indulgence of staying in an extremely elegant home. When you first see the sumptuous decoration of the reception rooms at Tílias it is hard to believe that José found the house a near ruin and needed two long years to return things to the way they were. Although you are in an attractive small town, the high wall surrounding the gardens creates a mood of peaceful privacy. The house's most remarkable feature is the corniced and painted 'empire' ceiling of the first-floor lounge, where Santa Rainha Isabel gazes down on shining parquet, card table, period dresser and old prints, evoking the Portugal of yesteryear. The dining room is also a grand affair with chandelier, family china, silver service and an elegant table decoration at breakfast (when you can try the local cheese and honey). The bar has a much more rustic, relaxed mien with exposed granite and wood burner; try the local *aguardente* (grape liqueur) on a cold night. Wood-panelled corridors take you to the guest bedrooms which are large, airy, prettily decorated and look out to the garden.

**Rooms:** 6 with bath or shower & wc; 1 suite.
**Price:** Double/Twin Esc 12,500; Suite Esc 14,000.
**Breakfast:** Included.
**Meals:** Only for groups on request.
**Closed:** Never.

From Porto A1 towards Lisbon, then IP5 to Viseu. Into centre then to Seia via Nelas. Here in town centre follow sign for São Romão for 2km. Signposted.

**Map no: 1**

# Quinta da Geía
3400-214 Aldeia das Dez
Beira

**Tel:** 238 670010
**Fax:** 238 670019
**E-mail:** quintadageia@mail.telepac.pt
**Web:** www.quintadageia.com

### Fir Tiebout

Aldeia das Dez in the foothills of the Serra da Estrela, is an old hamlet to which the 20th century seems only to have given a passing glance. From the outside you'd never guess that the house is several hundred years old: Dutch Frans and Fir have completely renovated the place. Life at Quinta da Geía centres on the lively bar and restaurant. It has stained wooden tables and chairs, bright tablecloths, paintings by local artists and is well frequented by the local folk who obviously approve of the cooking; Frans describes it as "trad Portuguese with a difference", the difference being an Italian/French slant in the preparation of sauces and veg. Once a week bread is baked in the original brick oven. Bedrooms are large, light and functional; they have pine floors, interesting angles and are beautifully finished. A suite or apartment would be perfect for families. Your hosts have mapped out the best walks in the area; follow ancient (Roman) pathways through forests of oak and chestnut. An exceptional place, now with two large conference rooms. *Minimum stay of 1 week in summer in apartments or 3 nights rest of year.*

**Rooms:** 15 from standard to suites;
3 apartments.
**Price:** Esc 9,500-17,500
Apts (4 people) Esc 13,500-17,200
Apts (6 people) Esc 18,000-20,000.
**Breakfast:** Included in price of rooms, not apartments.
**Meals:** Lunch/Dinner Esc 3,200.
**Closed:** January 2-22.

From Coimbra take N17 towards Guarda. About 10km before Oliveira do Hospital, at Vendas de Galizes, right at sign for 'Hotel Rural'. Follow signs for 14km.

Map no: 1

# Quinta do Rio Dão

3440-464 Santa Comba Dão
Beira

**Tel:** 232 880240
**Fax:** 232 880249
**E-mail:** quinta@quintadoriodao.pt
**Web:** www.quintadoriodao.pt

### Pieter & Juliette Gruppelaar-Spierings

The setting is a dream, with the house almost hidden in a stand of old oaks right
on the bank of the river Dão at the very point where it opens out to form a small
lagoon. Pieter and Juliette, friendly hosts both, came across the farmhouse when it
stood in ruins and have sensitively restored it and the neighbouring buildings in
traditional Beira style. They offer you the choice of a room, an apartment or a
whole house: the common threads are a beautiful use of wood, big verandas and
captivating prospects down towards the river. Pieter and Juliette have married
traditional Portugal with a clean, uncluttered (and Dutch) approach to space: there
is nothing too showy to detract from the sheer pleasure of being here. In summer
life is spent mostly outdoors; breakfast on the veranda to birdsong and dine on
traditional Beira dishes at night with the lights of nearby Santa Comba Dão
reflected in the water. Rooms and food are marvellous value; there are canoes, a
rowing boat and a windsurfer for guests to use. Pets can be housed, but not in the
rooms. Our inspector loved her stay: "In a word, idyllic". This is just the place for
a really energising holiday and children would love it too.

**Rooms:** 4 with bath & wc; 2 apartments
(sleep 2-4) and 3 cottages (sleep 4-8).
**Price:** Double/Twin Esc 8,500-12,000;
Apartment Esc 8,500-12,000; Cottages
(for 4-6) Esc 15,000-22,500, (for 8) Esc
25,000-29,500.
**Breakfast:** Included in price of rooms.
**Meals:** Dinner, 3-course, Esc 2,800.
**Closed:** Never.

From Lisbon towards Porto on A1 then after Coimbra turn to Viseu/Figueira da
Foz on the IP3 to Viseu. 500m before Santa Comba Dão turn to Vimieiro. Follow
the sign 'Agro Turismo' until the quinta (4.5km).

**Map no: 1**                                    Entry no: 56

# Solar da Quinta

Póvoa dos Mosqueiros      **Tel:** 232-891708
3440-458 S. João de Areias      96 400 8077 (mob)
Beira      **Fax:** 232 892382

### António & Susanna Antunes

Immense granite walls and beautiful woodwork add to the charm of this superb
17th-century manor house. The friendliness of António and his wife Susanna is an
added bonus. The house has been very well restored yet retains a great atmosphere
drawn from its long history. The bedrooms are cosy, with beds of iron and wood
and are all decorated in the characteristic rustic style; you sleep well here. The
bathrooms are a good size and finished to a high standard. Breakfast is served in
the large open kitchen, and do try Susanna's delicious evening meals. Receptions
rooms in the house are beautiful, with wooden ceilings and fine wood furniture.
Heavy wooden doors are set into stone walls and in one corner of the lounge is a
massive granite boulder – it's part carved and part foundation. Outside is a yard,
bordered by thick granite walls and Susanna's organic vegetable garden and
'garden of aromas', where you can relax with a drink and enjoy the scent of
honeysuckle, rose, jasmine and herbs. All around, mammoth rounded granite
boulders protrude from the turf, one carved into a flowform. A friendly house
with lots of character and good food.

**Rooms:** 5 with bath & wc.
**Price:** Double/Twin Esc 12,500; Single Esc 10,000
(min. 2 nights).
**Breakfast:** Included.
**Meals:** Lunch/dinner available by arrangement.
**Closed:** Never.

From the IP3 Coimbra-Viseu road leave at km79 Rojão
Grande; from there follow the signs Póvoa dos
Mosqueiros 2km away. The house is in the centre of the
village.

Entry no: 57          **Map no: 1**

# Casa da Azenha Velha

Caceira de Cima
3080 Figueira da Foz
Beira

**Tel:** 233 425041
**Fax:** 233 429704

**Maria de Lourdes Nogueira**

Once a flour mill (*azenha*), this large house is now much more: the decorative flourishes above doors and windows and large rooms suggest a rather grand history and after Maria de Lourdes and her two dogs have met you, you will find that the grounds support plentiful deer, ostriches, cows and peacocks. The bedrooms and apartment are separate from the main house and have been decorated with great attention to detail and colour-co-ordination; even tiles match the fabrics and there are large sunken baths. They are excellent value. You breakfast in the large kitchen of the main house; rail-sleepers support the roof-bricks, an original and attractive feature. Here too is a snug living room with leather sofas, a hearth and lots of ornaments. There's a large lounge in the old stable block with an honesty bar. The Azenha is well geared for family visits: as well as the animals which children will love, there are plenty of board games, snooker table, pool, tennis court and six horses to be ridden. Not far from the main house is the new, rustic-style Azenha restaurant where you eat regional and international dishes.

**Rooms:** 5 with bath & wc;
1 apartment for 4.
**Price:** Double/Twin Esc 13,000;
Apartment Esc 20,000.
**Breakfast:** Included.
**Meals:** Restaurant in the house.
**Closed:** Never.

From Coimbra N111 towards Figueira da Foz. Shortly before arriving there turn off towards Caceira and then immediately left following signs 'Turismo rural'. After about 2km right and after 500m right again. House on left.

**Map no: 3**

**Entry no: 58**

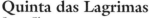

# Quinta das Lagrimas

Santa Clara
Apart. 5053
3041-901 Coimbra
Beira

**Tel:** 239 802380
**Fax:** 239 441695
**E-mail:** hotelagrimas@mail.telepac.pt
**Web:** www.supernet.pt/hotelagrimas

**Mario Morais**

Quinta das Lagrimas has a place among the most remarkable hostelries in
Portugal, perhaps in Europe. The Palace is 300 years old but was rebuilt after a fire
a century ago. Wellington stayed here and was captivated by the place and the
legend that the tears (*lagrimas*) of the name were those shed by Dona Inês when
put to the dagger by the knights of King Alfonso. Come to see 10 acres of
wonderful gardens to which species have been brought from all over the world;
two giant sequoias were a gift from the Iron Duke himself (hence *Wellingtonia*).
The elegance of the double sweep of staircase leading up to the main front is
mirrored within. The dining room is stuccoed, panelled and chandeliered;
dignitaries are international but the the food is Portuguese and accompanied by
fine wines from Lagrima's large cellars. Bedrooms are fit for kings (a number have
stayed here); they are elegant and deeply luxurious with rich fabrics, vast beds and
marbled bathrooms. The 'normal' rooms are anything but normal; the suites to
write home about. There is a colonnaded swimming pool, a snooker room for a
post-prandial game and interesting works of modern art.

**Rooms:** 35 with bath & wc; 4 suites.
**Price:** Double/Twin Esc 24,000-31,000;
Suite Esc 60,000-75,000.
**Breakfast:** Included.
**Meals:** Lunch/Dinner approx.
Esc 7,000-10,000.
**Closed:** Never.

Just outside Coimbra, behind 'Portugal dos
Pequenitos', take EN1 as if going to
Lisbon, and turn off to the right at the
hotel sign.

# Casa Pombal

Rua das Flores, Nº 18
3000-442 Coimbra
Beira

**Tel:** 239 835175
**Fax:** 239 821548

### Else Denninghoff Stelling

Built on hills overlooking the river Mondego, Coimbra is a city to explore slowly; once capital of the (young) nation it is most famous for its very ancient university; try to visit in term time when the students add so much life to the city. At the heart of Coimbra, among narrow streets on a hill close to the famous seat of learning, the Casa Pombal is delightful; friendly, utterly unpretentious, it will stir feelings of nostalgia for those student years. Four of the rooms have breathtaking views over the old city roofscape and down to the Mondego river. They are basic but very clean and comfortable; three have their own bathrooms, but sacrifice a little luxury for the sweeter pleasures of those views and the relaxed atmosphere created by the friendly Dutch owners, who are very willing to give lots of local information. It is better to book in advance, and single folk will especially enjoy this place, where they're bound to meet fellow travellers over breakfast (eggs, cereals, fresh juices and home-made jams) or in the small courtyard. Pets are allowed in rooms but not the common room or patio. *Pombal* is the Portuguese for dovecote and this old town house certainly got us cooing.

**Rooms:** 3 with bath & wc and 7 sharing bathrooms & wcs.
**Price:** Twin Esc 7,000-8,500; Double/Twin (sharing bath & wc) Esc 5,500-7,200.
**Breakfast:** Included.
**Meals:** Dinner for groups (min. 4), on request Esc 2,900.
**Closed:** Mid-December-mid-February.

In Coimbra follow signs 'Universidad' via Avenida Sá da Bandeira then towards Praça da Republica; last right just before the Praça (don't go as far as the University), right again on Rua Padre António Vieira. Park as close to end of street as possible. If lost ask for Rua da Matemática.

**Map no: 3**

Entry no: 60

# Casa Dona Jerónima
3230-341 Penela-Coimbra          **Tel:** 239 561180
Beira                                          **Fax:** 239 561179

**Eveline Schripsema**

Hidden in a fold of the hills near historic Penela, far from road and traffic, this special home looks down a sheltered valley, and is a perfect place to get away from it all. Eveline, a former philosophy teacher, loves literature and has a holiday home with a difference: as well as a good library, she has sculpted her garden so as to create several secluded places where you can sit can and read. She rebuilt these two old farm houses a few years ago and all is now modernised – and light. The twin rooms are different in shapes and sizes, decorated in rustic style with Alentejo rugs over tiled floors and crewel bedcovers and curtains. All of them have views out to the surrounding trees and vineyards; aromas of orange blossom and the song of birds drift in through their windows. The house has a split-level breakfast room with a long communal table and a lower lounge; it leads to a terrace where guests can eat or sit and abandon themselves to the peace of the place. Walking possibilities abound and Coimbra and Tomar are not far away. But Eveline hopes that her guests will appreciate above all having the space to slow to Dona Jerónima's slower, deeply rural rhythms.

**Rooms:** 3 twins and 1 triple, all with bath & wc.
**Price:** Twin Esc 7,500-12,500.
**Breakfast:** Included.
**Meals:** Light lunch & dinner available.
**Closed:** Never.

From Coimbra, take the IC3 and, while passing Penela, watch for small sign to the right 'Infestos'. Turn onto the track and keep going. At white wall turn right, keep going, and find house after 3km.

# Casa no Céu

Vale Pereira da Serra
3200-128 Lousã
Beira

**Tel:** 239 994 168
**E-mail:** traduz@mail.telepac.pt
**Web:** www.portugalholidayvillas.homestead.com

**James Lawrence**

The 'House in the Sky' is reached by a steep climb – it's well worth the effort. High up on a north-west, forested hillside, the air is pure and there are wonderful views of rolling hills and the neighbouring hamlet where James lives. The self-catering house was once a goat shed, but the conversion has been beautifully done and now this is a perfect getaway place for two. There are grassy terraces and flowerbeds around the house and a stone terrace with tables, chairs and barbecue. The L-shaped bedroom is built into the hillside so that rocks form part of the walls – it has a wooden floor and comfortable mahogany double bed. The dining room and kitchen area has a big fireplace (logs are provided when needed) and there's a hi-fi, so bring your music. When you arrive James will present you with a generous hamper with dozens of cooking ingredients plus bottles of red and white wine and beer. There are two mountain bikes and those fond of walking can follow the path to Lousã castle; there is also a stunning gorge with waterfalls and swimming places nearby. James even lends you a mobile phone so that if you get lost on your rambles through the forest you can phone for help!

**Rooms:** 1 with shower & wc.
**Price:** Double/Twin Esc 13,000; Apartment Esc 20,000.
**Breakfast:** Self-catering.
**Meals:** Self-catering.
**Closed:** Never.

A map is mailed to guests. From the IC3 Tomar-Coimbra towards Penela turn right to Espinhal, and at Miranda do Corvo turn right to Espinhô. Keep going through Espinhô and Cova do Lobo, to Levegada. Just after Café Pim Pim take small track to right and keep going until you're almost in the sky.

**Map no: 3**

# Casa do Cimo

Aldeia Nova do Cabo       **Tel:** 275 771431/243 324991
6230-050 Fundão
Beira

**Judite & Jõao Miguel Miranda da Câmara Vasconcelos Alvaiazere**

Grand, gracious, grandiose... the Casa do Cimo is all these and more. The house, festooned with Virginia creeper, was built in 1578 and has belonged to the same noble family ever since. Much has happened here over the centuries, and you'll see the family coat of arms over the entrance, over the fireplace and embroidered in colour on the towels. This large, cream, granite building, sited at the top of the village, has superb views of the Serra da Estrela mountains behind. The dining room, sitting room and halls are all magnificent, with stone walls, large stone arches, vast fireplaces and wooden ceilings, and are all superbly decorated. Most of the bedrooms are very grand, with high ceilings and beautifully crafted antique furniture. All the rooms have something special in terms of their finish and furnishing. Breakfast is self-service in the lovely old kitchen and is delicious with freshly squeezed orange juice and home-made jams. Outside there is an attractive garden, a *tanque* – where you can take a quick dip – fed by spring water, those views, plus the cobbled streets of the village at the front. Come for the grandeur and the peace.

**Rooms:** 10 with bath & shower & wc;
1 suite.
**Price:** Double/Twin Esc 15,000; Single
Esc 12,000; Suite Esc 20,000.
**Breakfast:** Included.
**Meals:** Dinner Esc 4,000, by arrangement.
**Closed:** Never.

From the IP2 Castelo Branco-Guarda road turn to Fundão. Go straight through Fundão until old church, sign Aldeia Vona and Silvaras; go to Silvaras and after 2km turn right at sign for Aldeia Nova do Cabo. House on left as you reach village.

# Casa do Castelo Novo

Rua Nossa Senhora das Graças – 7
6230-160 Castelo Novo
Beira

**Tel:** 275 561373
**Fax:** 275 561373
**E-mail:** castelonovo@yahoo.com

**Alice Aleixo**

A 17th-century home on the slopes of the Serra da Gardunha, an amphitheatre of green tones which leads down to the winding lanes of the village. The front of this elegant house, with its wonderful granite stonework, is deceptive, because you cannot guess how the house is built up the steep rock, and that the garden is at the level of the first floor. The ground-floor is a sitting room for guests, where there are sofas, a wall of rock, and carpets from the Minho and Morocco; there's a small table too where you can breakfast. Go up a wooden staircase and you find the main living room; here there are sofas, a granite fireplace, bookcases cut into the stone walls, displays of ceramics, antiques and a shell-like wooden *maceira* ceiling above. The mountain view from the corner window is wonderful. The dining/breakfast room is cosy, 19th-century style. In the main house are a bedroom and suite, both with *Dona Maria* beds – the latter has the best view in the house according to Alice. A few steps across the garden and you have a choice of a painted Alentejo double or Romantic twins. The garden is simple, flourishing... and what views!

**Rooms:** 3 with bath & wc; 1 suite.
**Price:** Double/Twin Esc 9-12,000; Suite Esc 12-14,000; extra bed Esc 3000.
**Breakfast:** Included.
**Meals:** Lunch/Dinner available with notice from Esc 2,500.
**Closed:** Never.

On the IP2, Castelo Branco to Fundão. Nearing Fundão look for signs to Castelo Novo. You enter village on Rua de São Brás; at Largo da Bica go right along Rua da Gardunha, around the castle, until it joins Rua Nossa Senhora das Graças; go across Largo Petrus Guterri, and follow signs to the house.

**Map no: 4**

# Albergue do Bonjardim

Nesperal
6100-459 Sertã
Beira

**Tel:** 274 809647
**Fax:** 274 809323
**E-mail:** albergbonjardim@mail.telepac.pt
**Web:** www.albergue-do-bonjardim.com

**Hubertus Johannes Lenders**

Eden-esque countryside laps up to this elegant 18th-century country house, approached along the narrowest country lanes flanked by vineyards and groves of orange, olive and almond. If you enjoy wine you should book at least a night at Bonjardim; the Lenders have a well-stocked cellar and there is a cosy bar for tastings of the estate's organic wine. The four guest bedrooms are just right: big, light rooms with pine floors, high ceilings, antique beds and dressers, and carefully chosen fabrics and colours. Two of them are in the main house and reached via a fine old granite staircase. The other two are in an outbuilding and, if booked together, can be joined to make an apartment for six; these have a south-facing veranda and there is a woodburning stove and the same light and uncluttered feel of the main house. The pool is indoors, along with a sauna and a Turkish bath. There are also a children's playground, ponies and horses to ride, canoeing nearby and good walks galore; but find time to visit the winery with Hubertus. He is a convivial host and runs courses which cover all aspects of wine. "An oasis of peace" wrote one guest, "Gateway to tranquillity," said another.

**Rooms:** 4 with bath & wc.
**Price:** Double/Twin Esc 12,500-14,000.
**Breakfast:** Included.
**Meals:** None available.
**Closed:** November 1-May 1.

From Coimbra, IC8 towards Castelo Branco and exit to Sertã. There N238 towards Tomar. At sign marking beginning of village of Cernache do Bonjardim, left at sign 'Nesperal-turismo rural'. Follow signs.

# Casa da Padeira

EN8 – S. Vicente
2460-711 Aljubarrota
Beira

**Tel:** 262 505240
**Fax:** 262 505241
**E-mail:** casadapadeira@mail.telepac.pt

**Lina Pacheco**

Casa da Padeira takes its name from the baker's wife of Aljubarrota who, so legend has it, single-handedly dispatched seven Spaniards. A frieze of *azulejos* (tiles) on the bar in the lounge shows her thwacking one of the septet into the bread oven. Several centuries on, a more gentle reception awaits you at this quiet guest house run by Lena and Nuno. The house is not old but the bedrooms on the first floor have a flavour of antique style thanks to ornately turned Bilros beds and furniture. The self-contained apartments (some with wheelchair access) are well furnished, with large double bedrooms, an additional sofa bed and attractive bathroom. The lounge has a wide stone fireplace for colder nights and capacious yellow-striped armchairs and sofa. You breakfast well at Padeira, with a selection of bread, cake, cheese and meat, and for further pleasure there is an excellent restaurant in nearby Aljubarrota. When you return after forays, visit the games room, with cheerful yellow/orange walls and pool table and other diversions. The Padeira garden also has a pleasant sheltered swimming pool bordered by plants, with sun-loungers, tables and chairs aplenty.

**Rooms:** 8 plus 6 apartments, with bath & wc.
**Price:** Double/Twin Esc 13,000; Apartment Esc 20,000.
**Breakfast:** Included in rooms; Apartment self-catering.
**Meals:** None available.
**Closed:** Never.

Along the EN8 from Alcobaça towards Batalha; the house is signposted on the left after leaving Aljubarrota.

Map no: 3

Entry no: 66

# Casa do Outeiro

Largo Carvalho do Outeiro, 4          **Tel:** 244 765806
2440-128 Batalha                      **Fax:** 244 765806
Estremadura

**José Victor Pereira Madeira**

The colossal Abbey of Batalha was built in thanks for Dom João's victory over the Castilian army in 1385 which secured the independence of Portugal. A masterpiece of Portuguese Manueline art, the exterior of the Abbey is all carved pinnacles, columns and buttresses; the innards, especially the cloisters, are exceptionally beautiful, too. Do stay at Outeiro if you come to visit, even if at first appearance it is a rather unexciting place. This small modern guesthouse is right in the centre of Batalha, its hillside perch ensuring that some bedrooms have views across the town's rooftops to the great Abbey. José and Odete are the best of hosts; both manage to combine careers in the town with attending to their guests. Their bedrooms are roomy and functional; all have modern pine furniture but their private terraces and size lifts them into the 'special' league. And the use of wood for floors and ceilings helps to add warmth to a modern building. Most of the area to the rear of the building is given over to the swimming pool. Your ever-helpful owners will advise you where to dine out and, in the morning, treat you to a generous breakfast that includes five or six home-made jams. Excellent value.

**Rooms:** 8 with bath & wc; 1 suite.
**Price:** Double/Twin Esc 8,000-11,000;
Suite Esc 8,000-11,000.
**Breakfast:** Included – Continental.
**Meals:** None available.
**Closed:** Never.

On arriving in Batalha follow signs for centre. The Casa do Outeiro is well signposted.

**Entry no: 67**                                      **Map no: 3**

# A Colina Atlântica

Quinta das Maças
Travessa dos Melquites, Nº3, Barrantes
2500-621 Salir de Matos
Estremadura

**Tel:** 262 877312
**Fax:** mobile: 96 7024958
**E-mail:** colinaatlantica@hotmail.com

**Ineke van der Wiele**

Meditation, tarot, reiki, communal meals... this is a house with its own special atmosphere and focus. Its 1950s exterior may look unprepossessing but the company is good and the mood informal. Ineke and her partner Ton, who have travelled a good deal in India and Asia, soon make you feel at home – it's a good place to come if you're travelling alone. The house's huge loft is now a beautiful meditation room with a wood-lined roof, cotton rugs and futons. Here you can combine spiritual interests with more earthly pursuits. If you'd like a knowledgeable escort, Ton will take you to the monasteries of Alcobaça and Batalha, to Óbidos and Nazaré. The bedrooms, in what once were the stables, have tiled floors and wooden ceilings; they are quite basic but comfortable. (There is also even more basic accommodation in caravans out in the large garden!) There's no maid service, so you clean your own room. Most nights there are communal 'world cuisine' dinners in the dining room which opens onto the pleasant garden with tinkling chimes. A friendly place which works its magic on many levels.

**Rooms:** 3 with bath & wc, 1 sharing bathroom; 3 caravans sharing bathroom.
**Price:** Per person: Esc 4,500;
Single Esc 4,500-6,500.
**Breakfast:** Included (as is guided meditation).
**Meals:** Dinner on request, Esc 2,000 inc. wine.
**Closed:** November-April (open Christmas & New Year).

From Caldas da Rainha towards Alcobaça. After 6km, at Tornada, turn right, to Barrantes. At end of village fork left at signpost to Valado; after 100m; right opp. new house; Colina is 50m on left under tall pines and cedars.

**Map no: 3**  Entry no: 68

# Casa do Casal do Pinhão

Bairro Sra. da Luz
2510 Óbidos
Estremadura

**Tel:** 262 959078
**Fax:** 262 959078
**E-mail:** casalpinhao@mail.pt
**Web:** www.caldas2000.com/casalpinhao

**Maria Adelaide**

Not far from the medieval town of Obidos, in pine forests and farmland, is this country retreat, a long modern house with bedrooms in a line overlooking the pool. It's a mixture of purpose-built-for-rural-tourism, family home and stud farm. Each 18th-century style bedroom has a different colour theme and *Dona Maria* beds with high headboards; the look is elegant and bathrooms are of high quality. The apartments here are large, very modern, Portuguese in style and well equipped. This is a place where you can climb out of bed, open the French windows, walk out and submerge yourself in the pool which is set into the terrace below (there's also a shallow one for children). You hear only the birds singing and perhaps sheep or goats and you can see the famous arch-necked Lusitanian horses in stables nearby. There are pine, oak and eucalyptus trees near the house, and a shady pergola where you can take a drink from the 'honesty' bar. Breakfast is self-service and Continental. Traditional Portuguese cooking is available in the evenings and there are interesting restaurants in the old streets of Óbidos. (There are two two-bedroom apartments 1km away at a neighbouring *quinta*.)

**Rooms:** 8 with bath & wc; 2 2-bed apartments and 2 1-bed apartments.
**Price:** Double/Twin Esc 12,000-16,000.
**Breakfast:** Included for rooms. Apartments self-catering.
**Meals:** Dinner on request, Esc 2,500-3,000.
**Closed:** Never.

On the EN8 from Óbidos to Caldas da Rainha & Tomar; look for blue signs to Casal do Pinhão.

# Casa de S. Thiago do Castelo

Largo de S. Thiago          **Tel:** 262 959587
2510-106 Óbidos            **Fax:** 262 959587
Estremadura

**Carlos Lopes**

Don't miss Óbidos, cradled by its very old (14th-century) wall. It is a beguiling maze of narrow cobbled streets softened by blue and ochre pastel washes and exuberant stands of bougainvillaea and jasmine. There are cameo views at every turn. The 'house of St James' has been in the family for over a century, though it was more recently that Carlos decided to throw it open to guests. A cheery French housekeeper welcomes you in; you'd never, from the outside, guess the extent of this old house. Decoration has been meticulously studied and carefully crafted. The bedrooms' most memorable features are massively thick walls (some windows are large enough for *conversadeiros* – gossiping seats!) and dark wood ceilings. There are wrought-iron bedsteads, matching prints for curtains and bedspreads, swanky bathrooms and details that you'd only expect of a larger hotel, like logo-ed writing paper and envelopes. On one level is a small lounge with open hearth; down below is a bar (try a glass of the local cherry liqueur *ginjinha*), a billiard room and, in the lee of the castle battlements, the most peaceful of patios for sitting out. Carlos enjoys exchanging anecdotes with his guests.

**Rooms:** 8 with bath & wc.
**Price:** Double/Twin Esc 16,000; New
Year/Easter/Carnival Esc 17,500.
**Breakfast:** Included.
**Meals:** On request. Prices vary.
**Closed:** Never.

On arrival in Óbidos enter town through main gate.
Continue to end of this street and house on right, just
below castle.

# Casa do Castelo
Estrada Nacional 114, Nº16
2520 Atouguia da Baleia
Estremadura

**Tel:** 262 750647
**Fax:** 262 750937

**João Paulo Horta Gama
d'Almeida Baltazar**

The Casa do Castelo is a 17th-century dream home whose walls embrace the ancient stones of the 12th-century castle walls. Maria and her piano-teaching husband João are a warm, charming and friendly couple who do all that they can to make you feel like one of the family. The house, striking with its pointed arched windows, has been faultlessly furnished. The bedrooms at the back of the main house are cosy and traditional and well furnished with Alcobaça bedcovers on the comfortable beds and heavy antique furniture. Three other bedrooms overlook the pool, and these are slightly less lavish in style, but no less harmonious. The sitting room is cosy, with an arched open fireplace – it's also the family room and is a perfect example of Portugal's *Turismo de Habitação* (home tourism). Breakfast is generous, and in season you drink orange juice freshly-squeezed from fruit on the trees outside the window. Lovely gardens surround the pool area – there's a 'dragon tree' by the entrance – and there's a games room, too.

**Rooms:** 7 with bath & wc.
**Price:** Double/Twin Esc 12,500-14,000;
Single Esc 10,600-12,500.
**Breakfast:** Included.
**Meals:** Dinner on request, Esc 2,500.
**Closed:** Never.

From Caldas da Rainha take the EN14 to Peniche. As soon as you reach Atouguia there is a big church on the left and Casa do Castelo is on the right as you come round the bend.

# Quinta de Santa Catarina

Rua Visconde da Palma d'Almeida    **Tel:** 261 422313
2530 Lourinhã    **Fax:** 261 414875
Estremadura    **E-mail:** quinta.santa.catarina@netc.pt

### Teresa Maria Palma de Almeida Braga

If style, elegance, comfort and service are high on your list of hotel essentials then Quinta de Santa Catarina is probably your type of place. It was built in the 16th century, rebuilt in the 18th and embellished by various illustrious forebears of the Almeida Braga family; they even escaped collectivisation during the Revolution. The expanding suburbs of Lourinhã have brought new neighbours but the building still looks out across wooded grounds where the tallest of palm trees (you'll find them on the family coat of arms too) increase the sensation of coming across a genuine oasis. You may be met by a uniformed maid who will lead you to your room via elegant reception rooms where ancestral portraits, gilded mirrors and chandeliers, brilliant polished tables and dressers, candelabras and flowers would all provide a wonderful backdrop for the grandest of weddings. That frisson of expectation is rewarded when the door of your room is pushed open and you are greeted by polished antique beds, dressers and occasional tables, more cut flowers, deep-pile carpets and captivating views out to the palm trees. Teresa teaches English and has a gift for making you feel immediately relaxed.

**Rooms:** 5 with bath or shower & wc.
**Price:** Double/Twin Esc 15,000-17,000;
Single Esc 12,000-15,000.
**Breakfast:** Included.
**Meals:** None, but snacks can be served by the pool.
**Closed:** December 24-25.

From Lisbon take A8 north towards Oporto then exit at junction 9 to Lourinhã; from here to the centre of Lourinhã and follow 'Turismo de Habitação' signs (close to Restaurante D. Sebastião).

**Map no: 3**      Entry no: 72

# Quinta da Barbara

Av. da Nossa Senhora da Esperança 303/305     **Tel:** 21 928 2678
2705 Fontanelas-Sintra                        **Fax:** 21 928 2597
Estremadura

**Maria Briscot**

It is rather different from most places you'll find in this book but Quinta da
Barbara could be just the place if you want to stay in one spot for a while; the
minimum stay here is three nights. The salmon-coloured houses are set among
pine trees in a corner of the Sintra National Park, as peaceful and secluded a spot
as you could hope to find. Each house, built to give maximum privacy, has its own
diner/open-plan kitchen/lounge with open fireplace and three-piece suite. Each
has a private terrace with attractive dragon-toothed cobbles and a barbecue. The
kitchens are equipped with everything you may (or may not) need for self-catering;
there is even a dishwasher. Maid service can be arranged if you like, but towels and
linen are regularly changed. You share the large swimming pool (chlorine-free)
with other guests, as well as a clay tennis court. A marvellous spot: the sea, beaches
and cliffs are just a kilometre away, Sintra a short drive, Azenhas do Mar nearby
and Lisbon a comfortable day-trip.

**Rooms:** 5 houses.
**Price:** House (for 2) Esc 10,500-21,000;
House (for 4) Esc 15,500-28,500; House
(for 6) Esc 19,500-38,000.
**Breakfast:** Self-catering.
**Meals:** None available.
**Closed:** Never.

From Lisbon to Sintra on IC19. There take
N247 towards Colares. Here right to Praia
da Maças. Through village to north and
1km after Azenhas do Mar Quinta signposted on right,
before you reach Fontanelas.

# Quinta Verde Sintra

Estrada de Magoito, 84
Casal da Granja
2710-252 Sintra
Estremadura

**Tel:** 21 961 6069
**Fax:** 21 960 8776
**E-mail:** mail@quintaverdesintra.com
**Web:** www.quintaverdesintra.com

**Cesaltina de Sena**

A modern house about midway between Sintra and the beaches, Quinta Verde Sintra is well away from the road, with distant green hills all around. This is a family home where Cesaltina, her husband Eugénio, and sons Miguel and André create an easy, friendly atmosphere. Nature is bountiful here and the house is wrapped around by honeysuckle, bougainvillaea, palms, bay trees, cedar and succulents. Inside, the sitting rooms have comfortable sofas, terracotta floors and typical Portuguese flourishes like a collection of plates on the walls. The suites have large sitting rooms and well-equipped kitchens. The mood here is modern and the bedrooms have a mixture of wooden and metal beds, tile floors with small rugs with matching fabrics on drapes and bedspreads; bathrooms are sparkling. Breakfast, a generous spread, is taken at the tables-for-two in the breakfast room, with its large fireplace at one end, or out on the terrace, looking out to the lush Sintra hills; see if you can pick out the Moorish castle, Pena Palace, Monserrate house, the Quinta da Regaleira and Palácio de Seteais.

**Rooms:** 5 with bath & wc; 2 suites.
**Price:** Double/Twin Esc 11,000-16,000; Suite Esc 13,000-19,000.
**Breakfast:** Included.
**Meals:** None available.
**Closed:** Never.

From Sintra look for signs to Várzea de Sintra/Magoito close to the Modern Art museum. Follow this road and at Várzea de Sintra look for the Restaurant Flor da Várzea and turn right. The Quinta is 1.5km further on.

Map no: 3

Entry no: 74

# Casa Pôr do Sol

Ulgueira                    **Tel:** 21 928 0354
Colares                     **Fax:** 21 928 0354
2705-349 Sintra
Estremadura

**Júlio José Filipe da Silva**

This sweet little self-catering cottage is at the bottom of a village in which the cobbled streets are all named after flowers. This is a true *casa portuguesa*, so there's a small patio to the rear for eating outside in summer, but no garden or patio in front. It has a comfortable feel, on a bijou scale, and the setting is peaceful – only one other household uses the road. For breakfast you'll find all you need in the fridge apart from bread which Maria, who lives next door, delivers daily to your back door. She is a good 'next-door neighbour', well-organised and very pleasant. The kitchen has pine-fronted cupboards and a good-sized table and the lounge, which has a woodburner and sofa-bed, is entirely cosy. There are 17th-century *azulejos* on the walls, and floors are terracotta. Bedrooms have wooden floors and ceilings and the furniture is all simple; one of them has a rather '40s feel. You can buy provisions for your meals in the village or dip into one of its restaurants – there are plenty of others along the coast. There are good local walks and the Adraga beach is 4km by car or a pretty 40-minute walk.

**Rooms:** 2-bed self-catering cottage.
**Price:** High season Esc 15,000, Esc 105,000 per week; Low season Esc 13,500, Esc 81,000 per week.
**Breakfast:** Included.
**Meals:** Self-catering.
**Closed:** Never.

From Sintra or Cascais, on EN247 to Ulgueira, and once in Viage take Rua das Flores down to the bottom of the village, and house is signposted to the right.

## Casa Miradouro
Rua Sotto Mayor, Nº 55
2710 Sintra-Vila
Estremadura

**Tel:** 21 9235900
**Fax:** 21 9241836
**Web:** www.casa-miradouro.com

**Frederico Kneubühl**

The gaily striped walls of Casa Miradouro make it an easy place to see as you wind down from Sintra. The present owner left a successful career in Switzerland to launch himself into restoring this light, elegant and airy home with views on all sides. Pass through a palm-graced porch and a handsome bannistered staircase leads you up to the bedrooms. Here antique beds and wardrobes rest on sisal floor matting; ceilings are high and have the original stucco mouldings. It feels fresh and uncluttered – helped by the size of the rooms – the two in the attic included. Views are to the sea or to the hills. The guest lounge has a similar unfussy feel; here the sisal balances less ethnic flounced curtains. There is a bar with several different ports – and a hearth for sitting round in the colder months. Further downstairs is a modern breakfast room, simply decorated with four round tables and giving onto a large terrace. Classical music accompanies breakfast: cereals, cheeses, juices, yoghurts, whatever fruit happens to be in season and both savoury and sweet breads. Frederico is a gentle-mannered, attentive and truly charming host, his home as well-manicured as any of Portugal's best.

**Rooms:** 6 with bath & wc.
**Price:** Single Esc 13,630-19,645; Double/Twin Esc 16,040-22,455.
**Breakfast:** Included.
**Meals:** None available.
**Closed:** January 6-February 23.

From Lisbon IC19 to Sintra. Here, follow brown signs for 'Centro Histórico'. At square by palace, right (in front of Hotel Central) and continue to Tivoli Hotel. There, down hill for 400m. House on left.

# Pensão Residencial Sintra

Quinta Visconde de Tojal          **Tel:** 21 923 0738
Travessa dos Avelares, Nº 12      **Fax:** 21 923 0738
2710-506 Sintra (S.Pedro)
Estremadura

**Susana Rosner Fragoso**

We loved the air of faded grandeur enveloping this family-run guesthouse. It was built on a thickly-wooded hillside as a Viscount's summer retreat in the days when fashionable Sintra was a hill station to local and international gentry – and became a guest house just after the war. An original bannistered staircase winds up to the first- and second-floor bedrooms. These are enormous with high ceilings, wooden floors and endearingly dated furniture and fittings; it all has a distinctly out-of-time feel about it. Ask for one of the two rooms with mountain views. Downstairs is an enormous dining room/bar where snacks are normally available, but we'd all prefer to sit out on the wide terrace (with tea and cakes in the afternoon) with its beguiling views up to the fairy-tale Moorish Castle. And the garden is a delight: dripping with greenery, and with some old, old trees, a swimming pool lower down and a small play area for children. Multilingual Susana is a young, bright and caring hostess. The village centre with its numerous restaurants and shops is a short stroll away or, for the more energetic, paths lead steeply up for some fine walks to Sintra's castles and palaces.

**Rooms:** 10 with bath & wc.
**Price:** Double/Twin Esc 8,000-16,000.
**Breakfast:** Included.
**Meals:** Snacks available all day.
**Closed:** Never.

From Lisbon IC19 towards Cascais. Exit for Sintra then follow signs for S. Pedro. Continue straight on through town. Hotel is signposted on right as you leave S. Pedro towards the historic centre of Sintra.

Entry no: 77                                      Map no: 3

# Quinta das Sequoias

Casa de Tapada
Estrada de Monserrate
2710 Sintra
Estremadura

**Tel:** 21 924 3821
**Fax:** 21 923 0342
**E-mail:** candigonzalez@hotmail.com

**Candida Gonzalez**

Hidden in its deep forest, this Quinta is steeped in seclusion, rich flora and dream-like views of fairy-tale palaces and castles. It is, as the poet Southey said of Sintra, a "blessed spot", and this long, two-storey white Quinta, dating from 1870, is full of delights. Candida, a retired doctor, has a home of remarkable beauty inside and out. Corridors and walls are replete with paintings and sculptures from some of Portugal's foremost artists, alongside fascinating older pieces from all over the world. The bedrooms are individual, with carved beds and polished mahogany furniture, rugs on tiled floors and carpets. The two bedrooms in the towers have beamed ceilings. The living room is long and large, with comfy sofas, and overlooks the garden. Nearby is a library, and both the games room (with bar) and breakfast room have wide windows. The breakfast room has a large open fireplace and tables large and small, and of course you can eat outside: Sintra is all slopes, and in front of the house the garden descends on lawned terraces, with pergolas and lush foliage, a burbling stream below and a swimming pool with views for miles. This quinta, the morning mists, sunrise and sunsets are indeed special.

**Rooms:** 5 all with bath & wc.
**Price:** Double/Twin Esc 13,000;
Apartment Esc 20,000.
**Breakfast:** Included.
**Meals:** Snacks and salads available.
**Closed:** Never.

From Sintra, follow the signs past the Tourist Office to Palácio de Seteais. Sequoias is signposted on the left, up 2km through the forest.

**Map no: 3**

**Entry no: 78**

# Hotel Central

Largo Raínha D. Amélia        **Tel:** 21 923 0963/4
2710-616 Sintra
Estremadura

**António Raio**

The insatiable wanderlust of Byron inevitably took him to Sintra, which he said was "the most beautiful village perhaps, in the world". It remains a spell-binding place, a romantic cocktail of greenery, magnificent views, and – see the Pena Palace, Moorish castle and Quinta de Regaleiros – fantasy, too. Right in the middle of what is now a small town is the Palácio Nacional, and right opposite is the Hotel Central. Our wintery photo of the façade does not really do it justice; in summer it is a wonderful place to sit out and people-watch. In days gone by the tea rooms were a place to be seen during the season. The whole hotel retains a distinctive 1900s feel. It can no longer be described as luxurious with its darkening 1940s tables and chairs and occasionally creaking floorboards, but the rooms are high-ceilinged, clean and agreeable. We enjoyed our breakfast and lunch in the light, parquet-floored dining room, under palms and Art Deco-style windows. If you want to stay right at the heart of things, the Central lives up to its name. Try to book the suite: it costs only a little more.

**Rooms:** 10 with bath & wc, and 1 suite.
**Price:** Double/Twin Esc 12,000-16,000; Single Esc 11,000-13,000; Suite Esc 14,000-17,000.
**Breakfast:** Included.
**Meals:** Lunch/dinner from Esc 3,500.
**Closed:** Never.

From Lisbon to Sintra on the motorway/N249. There to the centre, and hotel is on the main square by the Palácio Nacional.

Entry no: 79                              **Map no: 3**

# Quinta da Paderna

Rua da Paderna, 4
2710-604 Sintra
Estremadura

**Tel:** 21 923 5053
**Web:** planeta.clix.pt/paderna

### Maria Paixão

Just below the centre of Sintra, on a bend on a quiet cobbled street, is this unforgettable family-run guest house, a 19th-century villa full of character. This is the home of a lady of considerable energy and great warmth. Its halls, living room and dining rooms are decorated with family and religious pictures: Maria Paixão has, among other things, a deep interest in the spiritual life. She has created a garden temple to deities in her lush semi-wild grounds, where services are held every Sunday. Here you will see figures of many gods and gurus. From the garden there are views of the lush hills of Sintra, and a thousand shades (at least) of green. The bedrooms are quite small and simply decorated, but the furniture is good and the iron beds comfortable. Guests get their own breakfasts which can be eaten either in the dining room, with its huge dish-lined dresser or on the terrace – or you can walk up and breakfast in one of the cafés on the town's delightful main square. It may sound simple but such is the secure, family atmosphere, and sense of belonging and freedom, that guests come back year after year.

**Rooms:** 5 with shower & wc.
**Price:** Double/Twin Esc 13,000; Apartment Esc 20,000.
**Breakfast:** Self-catering.
**Meals:** None available.
**Closed:** Never.

From Lisbon to Sintra on the motorway/N249. There to the centre, and turn right by the Hotel Tivoli and Palácio Nacional, then continue down the steep Rua Soto Maior and take the second left into the Rua da Paderna; house is on the left on a hairpin right bend.

**Map no: 3**

**Entry no: 80**

# Estalagem do Forte Muchaxo

Praia do Guincho      **Tel:** 21 487 0221
2750 Cascais       **Fax:** 21 487 0444
Estremadura

**António Muchaxo**

Guincho is a long, curving sandy beach, backed by the Serra de Sintra, and a perfect place to watch Atlantic sunsets. One of the best views is from Tony Muchaxo's inn, perched at one end of the beach. It's full of character, a fantastic combination of ocean liner and Neptune's grotto, with lots of stone, cork pillars, strange wooden ceilings and floors of *calçada*, parquet, slate, terracotta and marble, often sloping to adjust for the fact that it was all built on the the ruin of an old fort. The restaurant has great views of the Atlantic, and the building is arranged around an inner courtyard where seabirds land among the succulents; outside there's plenty of peeling paint, but then the Guincho ocean is fierce. There are lots of plants inside, too, and in the bar a wishing well with running water, rock 'booths' and tree-trunk tabletops and pillars. Bedrooms are large and comfortable; choose one with sea views. You feel you're almost in the brine, and you hear the raging waves all night; an extraordinary mixture of wild nature, marble floors and beds with vinyl padded bed heads. Eat in or sample the many seafood restaurants along the coast and in cosmopolitan Cascais.

**Rooms:** 50 with bath & wc.
**Price:** Double/Twin Esc 10,000-26,000 (with sea view); Esc 8,000-18,000 (without).
**Breakfast:** Included.
**Meals:** Dinner available from Esc 4,000.
**Closed:** Never

In Cascais follow signs to Guincho. Drive along coast until you come to wide beach as road turns inland. Fort Muchaxo is on the curve on the left, a little below the road.

Entry no: 81          Map no: 3

# Casa da Pérgola

Avenida Valbom, Nº13
2750-508 Cascais
Estremadura

**Tel:** 21 484 0040
**Fax:** 21 483 4791
**E-mail:** pergolahouse@netc.pt
**Web:** ciberguia.pt/casa-da-pergola

**Patricia Gonçalves**

Old Cascais remains a fishing village, although holidaymakers and a growing number of Lisbon commuters have added a veneer of sophistication. Duck into the narrow, cobbled side-streets to find the old town and those cameo views for the camera. Casa da Pérgola reveals the days before the changes; the optimism of the belle époque is reflected in this grand villa's colourful façade with its red window surrounds, purple tiles and a cloak of white, orange and mauve bougainvillaea. Not a building that you'd miss as you wander by. Once inside, things take on a more subdued note: pastel colours, marble and antiques. In the upstairs lounge there are old paintings, pillars, elegant occasional tables and a grandfather clock whose gentle tock-tocking (paradoxically) makes it all feel slightly out-of-time; there is a faint whiff of a British seaside hotel. Bedrooms are all named after flowers, apart from one known as *Angels*. Those at the front are larger; some have balconies, some period beds, nearly all have fancy stucco cornicing and all a comfy chair. Throughout there are old prints (some of the saints) and the overall feel is more home than hotel. Particularly good value in the low season.

**Rooms:** 11 with bath & wc.
**Price:** Double/Twin Esc 14-18,000;
Double/Twin with balcony
Esc 16,000-20,000.
**Breakfast:** Included.
**Meals:** None available, except afternoon tea from Esc 550.
**Closed:** December 15-February 1.

From Lisbon A5 towards Cascais/Estoril. Exit for Abuxarda. Go to bottom of hill, turn right. At the third traffic lights turn left, at the next roundabout turn right. Pérgola is in the first street to left.

**Map no: 3**

## As Janelas Verdes
Rua das Janelas Verdes, 47
1200-690 Lisbon
Estremadura

**Tel:** 21 396 8143
**Fax:** 21 396 8144
**E-mail:** jverdes@heritage.pt
**Web:** www.heritage.pt

**The Cardoso & Duarte
Fernandes families**

Hidden away in the old city just yards from the Museum of Ancient Art, this old aristocratic town house (the great 19th-century novelist Eça de Queirós lived here) is a perfect place to lay your head when in Lisbon. From the moment you are greeted by the ever-smiling Palmira you feel like an honoured guest at As Janelas. Off to one side of reception is the lounge, complete with marble-topped tables (you breakfast here in winter), a handsome fireplace, piano and comfy chairs. You can breakfast on the patio (or have a candlelit aperitif); enormous ficus and bougainvillaea run riot, a fountain gurgles and wrought-iron tables stand on dragon-tooth cobbling. A grand old spiral staircase leads you to the rooms. Some have views down to the river (book early if you want one); they are furnished with repro beds, flounced curtains and delicate pastel colours. Dressing gowns and towels are embroidered with the JV logo. And instead of a 'do not disturb' sign you're provided with a hand-embroidered little pillow that says 'shhh!'. A delectable small hotel, recently enlarged to include a library on the top floor with impressive views of the River Tagus.

**Rooms:** 29 with bath & wc.
**Price:** Double/Twin 'Standard' Esc 24,700-33,500; Double/Twin 'Superior' Esc 30,500-41,500.
**Breakfast:** Not included.
**Meals:** None available.
**Closed:** Never.

A2 motorway across River Tejo then exit for Alcântara. Straight on at roundabout. Follow tram route for approx. 500m. Hotel close to Muséo de Arte Antigo on right.

# Hotel Britânia

Rua Rodrigues Sampaio, 17
1150-278 Lisbon
Estremadura

**Tel:** 21 315 5016
**Fax:** 21 315 5021
**E-mail:** britania.hotel@heritage.pt
**Web:** www.heritage.pt

### The Alves Sousa & Fernandes families

Just one street back from Av. de Liberdade, this gem of a hotel was designed by Cassiano Branco – it is a true museum-piece of '40s architecture and now ranks among Lisbon's classified buildings. The fun begins in the reception area which is flanked by twin ranks of marble columns; port-hole-windowed doors lead through to the bar, just the place for a Gin Sling. During recent renovation, paint was stripped away here to reveal what appears to be a sea-monster from Camoes' *Lusiades* (or there again, it may be Neptune); and there's more to be discovered. A wood and chrome staircase leads to the bedrooms (there's a lift too); these are generous, with their own private entrance halls. Bed, stools, chairs and writing table are all 'period', even if the fabrics look more modern and rather in the Laura Ashley vein. Bathrooms are also original, with huge sinks, tubs and marble walls. There's all the gadgetry that you'd expect of a three-star hotel (you may manage to bath without recourse to your tub-side phone). And if beds are period, mattresses are new. You can breakfast in your room – it's an enormous buffet that would probably keep you going all day.

**Rooms:** 30 with bath & wc.
**Price:** Double/Twin 'Standard' Esc 20,800-31,300; Double/Twin 'Superior' Esc 25,700-38,800.
**Breakfast:** Not included.
**Meals:** None available.
**Closed:** Never.

Follow signs to centre and Pr. Marquês de Pombal then towards Praça dos Restauradores. Left just before Metro 'Avenida'. Rodrigues Sampaio one street east of Av. de Liberdade.

**Map no: 3**                                   Entry no: 84

# Hotel Lisboa Plaza

Travessa do Salitre, 7
Av. de Liberdade
1269-066 Lisbon
Estremadura

**Tel:** 21 321 8218
**Fax:** 21 347 1630
**E-mail:** plaza.hotels@heritage.pt
**Web:** www.heritage.pt

**The Fernandes family**

Right at the centre of things and yet shielded from traffic noise this big, comfortable hotel has one of the best locations in Lisbon. The city's main attractions are all within easy reach and whenever you want you can slip back into the Plaza's calm, air-conditioned peace, irrespective of whether it's baking hot outside or, as does happen in Iberia, bucketing with rain. The hotel dates from the 1950s and the expansive public rooms are well designed with colour-co-ordinated fabrics and walls, plenty of marble floors and rugs. It's everything you expect a capital hotel to be – the style is understated and harmonious rather than particularly individual – but the attention and care you receive from staff is an enexpected bonus: they are courteous, professional and efficient, and most speak excellent English. The colour-themed bedrooms have comfortable twin beds and the excellent bathrooms have much marble and good-sized mirrors. The breakfast buffet will suit most tastes, as will the *Buffet da Quinta* restaurant food, though there are dozens of other restaurants to sample near the main Avenida.

**Rooms:** 94 rooms with bath & wc, and 12 suites.
**Price:** Double/Twin 'Standard' Esc 24,700-31,300; Double/Twin 'Superior' Esc 30,500-38,800.
**Breakfast:** Not included.
**Meals:** Lunch/dinner in restaurant, buffet or à la carte.
**Closed:** Never.

Go down the central Avenida de Liberdade, and at the War Memorial turn right into the Travessa Salitre. The hotel is 20m from the Avenida.

Entry no: 85

Map no: 3

## Residencial Florescente

Rua das Portas de Santo Antão,
Nº 99
1150 Lisboa
Estremadura

**Tel:** 21 342 5062/342 6609
**Fax:** 21 3427733

**Jacinta Antunes**

Another of the bright and cheerful family-run guesthouses that we are happy to include alongside some rather grander neighbours. Over many years, Florescente has built up a reputation as a friendly, clean and fun stopover right at the heart of Pombaline Lisbon. You are brilliantly central yet spared the rumble of traffic; Santo Antão is a pedestrianised thoroughfare and a great place to sit out at a café or restaurant and watch the world go by. You dip in off the street into the small tiled reception area; a small fountain gurgles in the corner and the young staff are immediately attentive. The original bannistered and tiled staircase, more than a century old, leads up and up... and up. Narrowish corridors lead to the bedrooms which are mostly medium-sized and simply decorated with a very southern choice of print on the walls. There are high-ceilings with stucco mouldings – a reminder of a more illustrious past. We loved the rather smaller attic rooms with their stand-up balconies, well worth the haul up to the fifth and top floor. No meals here, but just step outside and choose your café, restaurant or fruit shop. Ask for an air-conditioned room in the summer.

**Rooms:** 37 with bath & wc, 15 with shower & wc and 9 suites.
**Price:** Double/Twin Esc 5000-10,000; Suite Esc 14,000-16,000.
**Breakfast:** None available.
**Meals:** None available.
**Closed:** Never.

Arriving in Lisbon, follow signs into centre; down Avenida de Liberdade and park near Rossio in Restauradores car park.
Residencial in pedestrian street parallel to Liberdade, approx 100m to north of Rossio. Nearest Metro: Restauradores.

**Map no: 3**

# Residencial Alegria
Praça da Alegria 12
1250-004 Lisbon
Estremadura

**Tel:** 21 322 0670
**Fax:** 21 347 8070
**E-mail:** mail@alegrianet.com
**Web:** www.alegrianet.com

**Felix Santos**

This family-run guest house could hardly be in a better position, just yards away from the street-life of the Avenida de Liberdade yet in a quiet palm-graced square which seems to belie its inner-city status. At first glance the building looks a bit tatty but once you get inside you should approve of your room: "bright, cheerful, clean and basic" is how our inspector described her favourite Lisbon digs. For the moment there is not much in the way of public space but Felix, the Alergia's likeable owner, plans extend the ground floor into a larger breakfast room. Try to book our favourite room, number 114, which has been redecorated in a happy mix of blues and yellows (see photo); the double-glazing is good for light sleepers. Some rooms share bathrooms and a few are a shade drab with rather tired-looking bathrooms. But the corridors have been cleverly decorated in cheerful yellow and this and the shining parquet floors give the place a friendly atmosphere. An inexpensive and central address, close to restaurants and the capital's attractions, and ideal for the tighter budget.

**Rooms:** 40 with bath or shower & wc;
1 suite.
**Price:** Double /Twin with shower Esc 4,500-5,500;
Double/Twin with bath Esc 5,500-7,500; Suite Esc
5,000-6,000.
**Breakfast:** included.
**Meals:** None available.
**Closed:** Never.

Turn off Avenida de Liberdade into Praca de Alegria.
Residencial is between the police station and the
bombeiros, behind Hotel Sofitel. Nearest metro:
Avenida.

# Quinta de Santo Amaro

Aldeia da Piedade                **Tel:** 21 2189230
2925-375 Azeitão                 **Fax:** 21 2189390
Estremadura

**Maria da Pureza de O'Neill de Mello**

Looking out to the Arrábida mountains this genteel Quinta was where the de
Mello family would pass the summer months. Maria had fond memories of it all
from her childhood and later decided to make it her first home and bring new life
by opening her doors to guests. We loved the bedrooms and apartments because
of their deliciously homelike feel and each one is very different. For children there
is an attic with five beds. There are planked floors and ceilings in what is called 'the
middle house', attractive wooden beds here and in the apartment: wooden beds,
oil paintings and hearths, part-period bathrooms and a piano. When you arrive, it
is to a bottle of wine, and in winter to a log fire in the apartment. A wonderful
base for several nights; Lisbon is an easy drive, as are the beaches of the Setúbal
peninsula, and the local Fonseca wine cellars are well worth visiting. Breakfast is a
help-yourself feast of home-made breads, jams, cheeses, ham and freshly-squeezed
orange juice from Amaro's groves. But what makes it all so very special is Maria
herself, a lady with boundless enthusiasm and energy; heed her advice on where to
eat and what to visit.

**Rooms:** 5 with bath & wc; 1 apartment
with 3 bedrooms, all with bath & wc.
**Price:** Double/Twin (for 2) Esc 15,000
(min. 2 nights); Apartment (for 6) Esc
250,000 per week.
**Breakfast:** Self-service; kitchen available.
**Meals:** Self-catering.
**Closed:** Never.

From Lisbon, motorway towards Setúbal;
exit for Vila Nova de Azeitão. Here towards Sesimbra; after 3.5km, at Café Estrela
dos Arcos, take next left, 'Estrada dos Arcos'; S. Amaro is at the end.

**Map no: 3**                                              Entry no: 88

# O Moinho

Rua dos Aviadores, Nº69 R/C     **Tel:** 21 235 1033
2950 Palmela
Estremadura

**Paulo Costa Pereira**

If you've ever wanted to live in a windmill, here's your chance. Under the walls of
Palmela Castle, O Moinho is on a hill and has a wide-angle view of the world, of
olive trees and town below, of the hills and the distant sea. At night it's a vista of
twinkling lights – even the far-off power station looks rather enchanting! Within
this sturdy old windmill all tends to roundness; the workmanship and finish are
excellent, many old structural features have been kept and there are beams,
wooden floors and old stones. In the comfortable twin room, metal beds sit snug
beneath the building's cork-lined conical roof; a circle of stone blocks surmount
the thick, white-painted walls. It's cosy up here but on a blowy night you really
hear the wind; by day there are long views from the small square, low windows. A
steep, tricky stone staircase winds down to the circular living room where there's a
sofa bed and down another level is the kitchen/dining room with a central round
table; the kitchen cupboards and bathroom have been masterfully sculpted into the
room and there's also a woodburner. *The steep stairs would be dangerous for small
children.*

**Rooms:** 1 with shower & wc.
**Price:** For up to four people, Esc 12,000
per day (min. 3 nights); Esc 15,500 (2
nights).
**Breakfast:** Self-catering.
**Meals:** Self-catering.
**Closed:** Never.

From Setúbal go to Palmela, follow signs
for the Castelo and then 'Miradouro' – it's
the first of three windmills.

# Quinta do Salvador do Mundo

2590 Sobral de Monte Agraço       **Tel:** 261 943 198
Ribatejo                          **Fax:** 261 943 199
                                  **E-mail:** quintasalvador@ip.pt
                                  **Web:** www.quintasalvador.com

**Maria Theresa Sucena Paiva**

The Quinta of the Saviour of the World once belonged to the bishopric of Évora and is a large farmhouse near a Roman-Gothic church of the same name. This is an area of vineyards, rolling hills and windmills, and the farm overlooks a vast valley with views to the Serra do Socorro (Wellington's 'redoubt' was on the hill opposite during the Peninsular War). The quinta has been stylishly rebuilt, and is a stunning blend of old and new. It has grand furniture, a Steinway, chandeliers and silver, family antiques, and lots of glass and pine – all in alight and airy building. The furniture includes English, French, Portuguese and Indo-Portuguese pieces. Moroccan mosaic tables stand on a terrace outside the magnificent dining/breakfast room which has windows along one side and views of the valley and ruined church. The four bedrooms are in a separate building; they too are roomy and comfortable and all have antique beds and desks. Enjoy the luxury you'd expect in a top hotel, plus the grandeur of a *casa nobre* in a beautifully-designed modern setting. Maria is gracious, friendly and well travelled. *Five guests rooms in the main house are not generally available.*

**Rooms:** 4 with bath & wc.
**Price:** Double Esc 17,500-19,500; Single Esc 15,500-17,500.
**Breakfast:** Included.
**Meals:** Dinner Esc 3,500, by arrangement.
**Closed:** October 20-November 15.

From Lisbon, 26km on the A8, exit at Junction 6, left at Pero Negro; left again, then right, follow signs for Salvador (7 km from motorway).

**Map no: 3**

## Quinta das Covas

Cachoeiras
2600 Vila Franca de Xira
Ribatejo

**Tel:** 263 283031/ 33031
       96 510 3535 (mob)
**Fax:** 263 284543

**Susana Murschenhofer**

A Brazilian once owned this handsome manor and planted the garden with palms, medlars and some 20 varieties of orange tree. The house lies at the edge of the village of Cachoeiras surrounded by vineyards, orchards and fabulous gardens. Susana and Andreas fell in love with the place and somehow renovated, then decorated it all in just six months. No effort, or expense, was spared in creating an elegant, comfortable, luxurious and (occasionally) glitzy home. The most remarkable of the somewhat festive bedrooms is the *habitação do anjo*; it has a gold and blue Rococo bedroom set with a guardian angel carved into the headboard to hover over you as you sleep. *Portugal* has a palatial bathroom; another abandons tradition and has a wooden and steel bed supported on granite blocks: it's a copy of the one in the New York Museum of Modern Art. Our favourite was the one with its own private vine-festooned terrace. Best of all is the dining room with its original tiles and panelling: it leads to the terrace with a vine-covered pergola, a heavenly spot for breakfast or for afternoon tea (included in the price of your room). A bar and restaurant are planned in the Quinta's *adega*.

**Rooms:** 9 with bath or shower & wc.
**Price:** Double/Twin Esc 12,000-20,000.
**Breakfast:** Included.
**Meals:** Lunch/Dinner/Snacks
Esc 1,000-5,500.
**Closed:** Never.

From Lisbon A1 towards Porto then exit for Vila Franca. Then towards Cachoeiras following signs for Montegordo. Here first right to Quinta.

# Quinta da Ferraria

Ribeira de S. João
2040 Rio Maior
Ribatejo

**Tel:** 243 945001
**Fax:** 243 945696
**E-mail:** quinta.ferraria@mail.telepac.pt

**Teresa Nobre**

Quinta da Ferraria stands amid vineyards and olive groves; a channel cut from the nearby river powered the mill and ran a turbine powerful enough to light up the whole farm in the days before electricity arrived in Rio Maior. Recently the farm was totally renovated to create a handsome, small country hotel; although this has been set up for both business and pleasure, the exceptionally green and peaceful setting and the abundance of water make it special enough to please both types of guest. Gestors have pine floors and ceilings, soft Alcobaça fabrics and head-to-toe tiling in bathrooms. Pine is also the main feature of the sitting room; sisal matting, rugs and an open hearth add warmth to a very large space. The dining room, by contrast, felt rather soulless due to its wedding-banquet dimensions. But this is a good stopover, especially for a family; there are riding stables, and a farm museum. Next to the dining room you can still see the original olive-milling machinery. And, as the brochure points out, here are "blue-distanced horizons and clear, sparkling air to invigorate, stimulate and enhance life and living"!

**Rooms:** 12 with bath & wc, 1 suite & 2 apartments.
**Price:** Single Esc 15,500-16,100; Double/Twin Esc 18,200-19,200; Suite Esc 20,400-22,200, all inc. breakfast. Apartment Esc 25,900-28,400 (excl. breakfast); extra bed Esc 7,000-7500.
**Breakfast:** Included.
**Meals:** Lunch/Dinner on request, Esc 4,000.
**Closed:** December 24-25.

From Rio Maior N114 towards Santarem. The Quinta is signposted on right 8km from Rio Maior.

**Map no: 3**

Entry no: 92

# Casa do Foral

Rua da Boavista, Nº 10
2040 Rio Maior
Ribatejo

**Tel:** 243 992610
**Fax:** 243 992611
**E-mail:** moinhoforal@hotmail.com

### Carlos Higgs Madeira

This 19th-century town house is both pretty and unusual; outside it's attractive
because of its ivy-clad front, pebble cobbles and cast-iron porch. Inside it's unusual
because of the owner's pleasure in collecting, which has made it almost a museum.
Everywhere there are collections of some sort: of penknives, bottle-openers,
tankards, plates, fox-hunting prints and walking sticks. You will be looked after by
the friendly housekeeper Margarida. The house has a pleasantly quiet atmosphere
and the large, old-style lounge has plenty of sofas as well as collections of brass and
copper ware and old guns. The dining room has a rustic wooden table, leather
chairs, beams above and an old *azulejo* frieze. The breakfast room is modern and
minimalist – rather café-like – with wicker chairs, glass tables and a glass wall with
views of an interior courtyard and a lovely pepper tree. Outside are palms, oleander
and a rose pergola for shade. The pool is close to the beautifully designed modern
section. The bedrooms are comfortable and light with pine beheads and shutters
and lots of pale green; one has a glass wall and another a wooden mezzanine. A
house with a character all its own.

**Rooms:** 5 with bath & wc and 1 with
shower & wc.
**Price:** Double/Twin Esc 12,000; Single
Esc 9,000.
**Breakfast:** Included.
**Meals:** None available.
**Closed:** Never.

From the N1, Vila Franca/Santarem to
Caldas da Rainha. House signposted at the
northern end of Rio Maior. Turn right,
then right again, following Turismo de Habitação signs.

# Quinta do Vale de Lobos

Azoia de Baixo
2000 Santarém
Ribatejo

**Tel:** 243 429264
**Fax:** 243 429313
**E-mail:** valedelobos@mail.telepac.pt
**Web:** www.valedelobos.com

**Veronica & Joaquim Santos Lima**

Such is the veiled privacy of this old manor house that the Portuguese saying "to go to the Vale de Lobos" came to mean to go back to nature or to get far from the madding crowd. Nowadays, from the lush gardens, through the trees, you may just hear traffic in the distance but staying here remains a deeply restful experience. Veronica and Joaquim share their large home with four children, their housekeeper Cidalia and their guests. This much-travelled, polyglot couple receive you with great charm and their home is the sort in which most of us would love to live. Nothing superfluous or showy; elegant simplicity is the key note. The sitting room is light and cheery with striped curtains, deep sofas and an attractive wood and terracotta floor. There are books and magazines galore, mostly about things equestrian – you are in the Ribatejo, after all. We liked the bedrooms where the ornately turned *Bilros* beds, high ceilings, balconies and pretty bathrooms mirror the mood of the public rooms. The apartments are a treat, too; rather more modern in style, they have cleverly hidden kitchenettes and would be perfect for a longer stay.

**Rooms:** 4 with bath & wc; 2 apartments.
**Price:** Double/Twin Esc 16,000;
Apartment (2 adults & 2 children) Esc 19,000.
**Breakfast:** Included.
**Meals:** Lunch Esc 2,000, snacks also available;
by pool in summer!
**Closed:** December 23-31 .

From Santarém north on N3 towards Torres Novas. Through Portela das Padeiras, then just past turning for Azoia de Baixo cross a small bridge. Road turns left and climbs. As it bends right you turn left into the Quinta´s drive.

**Map no: 3**

Entry no: 94

# Quinta da Cortiçada

Outeiro da Cortiçada       **Tel:** 243 470000
2040 Rio Maior           **Fax:** 243 470009
Ribatejo

**Teresa Nobre**

Few settings are as utterly peaceful as that of Quinta da Cortiçada; this soft-salmon-coloured building, reached by a long poplar-lined avenue, sits in the greenest of valleys. As we arrived a heron rose from the lake and flapped slowly away, the sweetest of welcomes – so too was the gentle smile of the housekeeper who was waiting at the main entrance. Inside the building the silence feels almost monastic – birdsong instead of vespers. You have the choice of two lounges; one has a games table, high French windows on two sides and is dignified by the family *oratorio* (altarpiece). The other leads to a covered veranda with wicker tables and chairs. Where Cortiçada feels most homelike is in the dining room where, if you dine in, you'll rub shoulders with your fellow guests round the old oval table. Along the marble-paved corridor the rooms have old *Dona Mária* beds, antique dressers, thick rugs on the pine floors – and all of it is utterly pristine. Bathrooms are four-star plush, while sensitive lighting and carefully chosen fabrics help to make it all extra special. And, like that heron, you're welcome to fish in the lake.

**Rooms:** 6 with bath & wc; 2 suites.
**Price:** Single Esc 17,300-19,800;
Double/Twin Esc 17,300-19,800; Suite
Esc 23,500-25,900.
**Breakfast:** Included.
**Meals:** Lunch/Dinner on request,
Esc 4000.
**Closed:** Christmas Day.

From the A1, going north to Porto, exit at
Santarém/Rio Maior (EN114) and head
for Rio Maior. In Secorio, Quinta da Corticada is signed on right. After 12km, and
2km after Outeiro, you will see a pink farm in the valley.

Entry no: 95                                                **Map no: 3**

# Casa do Patriarca

Rua Patriarca D.José 134
Atalaia
2260-039 Vila Nova da Barquinha
Ribatejo

**Tel:** 249 710581
**Fax:** 249 710581
**E-mail:** mop59265@mail.telepac.pt

### Manuel d'Oliveira

This 500-year-old house has been the home of the d'Oliveira family for five generations. You may be greeted by Manuel's son, his daughter or his wife, as well as by two friendly boxers. The lounge has French windows leading to the walled garden. It is a long, low room, comfortable rather than grand, and a cool retreat in summer months. Just off it is a small kitchen for guests, a thoughtful touch for families not wanting to eat out. The long breakfast table is beautifully laid with home-made fruit and delicacies, and you can also have the full English version; in winter your juice will be fresh from Manuel's oranges. Bedrooms are delightful, each decorated to a different theme. *Quinta* has the great-great-grandfather's bed; *Oriente* has lamps and cushions from India, *Almirante* a naval theme and *Sana Sana* evokes Mozambique where your hosts spent their honeymoon. Outside, the huge gardens are a real pleasure. An enormous date palm towers above the pomegranate, medlar, orange and fig trees, there are shady spots to sit and relax, and a pool edged by trees. Manuel and his family are very caring people and staying here is a real treat.

**Rooms:** 6 with bath or shower & wc.
**Price:** Double/Twin Esc 10,000-15,000.
**Breakfast:** Included.
**Meals:** Self-catering.
**Closed:** Never.

From motorway Exit 1 for Torres Novas, then IP6, then IC3 for Tomar. After 1500m signposted for Atalaia and house.

Map no: 3                                    Entry no: 96

# O Palácio
2250-062 Constância            **Tel:** 249 739224
Ribatejo

### Maria José Themudo de Castro

The Tagus is wide as it winds past Constância, a small village of dipping streets. Indeed, there's almost a coastal feeling here, because of the promenades which run along by the waterfront. The Palácio is one of the biggest houses in the village, a gracious 19th-century villa which has long views of the river from its large bedrooms and terrace. The only dissonant note is a large paper mill which is just visible through the trees on the far bank – but it is too remote to be heard. Otherwise there is nature all around and the slow progress of the Tagus on its way to Lisbon and boats plying to and fro. The house is approached through gates into a courtyard, and inside you find yourself back in the world of 1885, of elegant polished furniture, period pictures, large rooms with high ceilings and decorative cornices, and an air of calm. The bedrooms are large, with long curtains and small balconies. At the back of the house is a long terrace, wrapped about by a magnificent, rambling wisteria; a perfect spot to sit and soak up the peace. At the front is the village, with its cafés and you are close to the Templar's castle at Almourol which stands on an island in the river – and to beautiful Tomar, too.

**Rooms:** 4 with bath & wc.
**Price:** Double Esc 11,500;
Single Esc 9,500.
**Breakfast:** Included.
**Meals:** None available.
**Closed:** December 10-27.

Going west on the IP6, past Torres Novas, look for signs for road to Constância Centro. Exit there and after about 1.5km you will find the Bombeiros (fire station). Turn left and look for the gates and courtyard of O Palácio.

## Pensão Residencial União

Rua Serpa Pinto 94
2300 Tomar
Ribatejo

**Tel:** 249 323161
**Fax:** 249 321299

Joaquim Farinha Rodrigues

Plumb on the main artery through the historic Templar town, under the castle battlements, this family-run pension was the town's very first hotel and recently celebrated its 106th birthday. The Gala dinners (see the scrapbook in reception) may no longer take place but the União remains the right choice in Tomar. A pretty tiled entrance beckons you in and up to the first floor reception and bar. Rooms are reached along corridors that twist and turn; easy to see why it took the painters six months to get round when last redecorating. The large dining room is where you are most in touch with the history of the building; tables and chairs are distinctly '40s whilst the door mouldings have an Art Deco air. High windows give onto the inner patio, a quiet spot to sit out when it's warm enough. The União's rooms, simple and with rather kitsch prints and a random mix of styles, are roomy with high ceilings, have very comfy beds and there is plenty of hot water. Rooms 102 and 103 were the best that we saw, with their old Italian lamps. No meals are served apart from breakfast so head out into the narrow backstreets of this lovely old town to sample one of the many restaurants. Book ahead in summer.

**Rooms:** 28 with bath & wc.
**Price:** Single 4,500 Esc; Double/Twin Esc 7,000; Triple Esc 8000.
**Breakfast:** Included.
**Meals:** None available.
**Closed:** Never.

Park as near to the centre as you can; the União is on the right hand side of the pedestrianised main street of 'Centro Histórico'.

**Map no: 3**

# Quinta da Alcaidaria – Mór

2490 Ourém
Ribatejo

**Tel:** 249 542231
**Fax:** 249 545034
**E-mail:** quinta.mor@netc.pt
**Web:** www.ciberguia.pt/qta-alcaidaria-mor

**The Vasconcelos Family**

This lovely wisteria-clad manor has been the family seat for more than 300 years and is every inch the grand country house: stately cedar-lined main drive, box-hedged gardens and its own private chapel. The main house is a cool, gracious building; light streams in to the high-ceilinged rooms while marble floors, arches and delicate plaster work remind you that you are in the South. Don't miss the chance to dine (remarkably inexpensive) around the enormous *pau santo* dining table. The chandeliers and collection of old china may inspire you to dress for dinner. Guest apartments are in a converted outbuilding; doubles are in the main house and most pukka they are too. There are old dressers, *Dona María* beds, comfortable chairs, perhaps a grand old tub with clawed feet; all rooms have beautiful moulded pine ceilings and big bathrooms and are generously tiled and marbled. Each is different from the next; all are first-class. Add to this the natural kindness of your English-speaking hosts (they often invite guests to join them for a glass of fine port) and you begin to get the measure of this altogether charming guest house.

**Rooms:** 5 with bath & wc; 2 suites.
**Price:** Double/Twin Esc 18,000-23,000; Suite Esc 18,000-23,000 (min. 3 night).
**Breakfast:** Included.
**Meals:** Light snacks & dinner on request, Esc 3,500.
**Closed:** Christmas & New Year.

From Ourém take Tomar road. After 2km left at fork towards Seica and then IMMEDIATELY left into cedar-lined avenue leading to house.

# Casa da Avó Genoveva

Rua 25 de Abril 16
Curvaceiras
2305-509 Tomar
Ribatejo

**Tel:** 249 982219
**Fax:** 249 981235

### José & Manuela Gomes da Costa

You are just outside beautiful Tomar and its Templar castle, but what first impresses you on arrival at Avó Genoveva is the serenity of the place. The huge old palm trees and pots of geraniums gracing the dragon-tooth courtyard, the soft salmon and white of the buildings give it a southern charm. José or Manuela usher you through to public rooms which are plush but homely; in the lounge there are family photos, woodburner, piano and card table while in the dining room there are antique dressers and a collection of old crockery – not a bit hotelly. You're spoiled for choice when deciding where to hunker down: in the music room feel free to put on a record (classical and *fado* in abundance), the snooker room doubles as a library and there is a small bar, well stocked with Portuguese wines. And what bedrooms! Dark pine ceilings, family antiques, old paintings; doubles are up an old stone staircase in the main house, while the apartments are across the way in the old granary. A respectable distance from the house are tennis court, swings and pool – and there are bikes, too. Your hosts are kindly, educated people who delight in sharing their wonderful home.

**Rooms:** 6 with bath & wc; 2 apartments.
**Price:** Double Esc 12,500; Apartment (for 2) Esc 15,000; Apartment (for 4) Esc 23,000.
**Breakfast:** Included.
**Meals:** None available.
**Closed:** Never.

From Tomar take road towards Lisbon. After approx. 9km in Guerreira turn right to Curvaceiras. After 4km house signposted on left.

**Map no: 3**

Entry no: 100

# Quinta do Troviscal

Alverangel – Castelo de Bode
2300 Tomar
Ribatejo

**Tel:** 249 371318
**Fax:** 249 371862
**E-mail:** troviscal@mail.telepac.pt
**Web:** www.troviscal.com

### Vera Sofia Castel Branco

If you love water, you'll love Troviscal, which looks out across the vast reservoir at Castelo de Bode; the Quinta offers peace, boating, swimming and long walks. Vera and João, who have three children, are a young, friendly couple, and their home is a modern, long-fronted villa at the edge of an inlet surrounded by tall pines, poplars and eucalyptus. The colours are the traditional yellow and white, the proportions are right, and inside there is a smooth blend of modern and traditional Portuguese style. In the bedrooms there is lots of wood, especially American oak, slate and tile floors and attractive hand-painted tiles. Beds are comfortable and all rooms open onto a long shaded terrace where breakfast is served. (A separate self-catering house is also available.) After breakfast you can walk down the terraces and through shaded pergolas, one a tunnel of wisteria, to the Troviscal's floating pontoon. All around is water and forest, and maybe an eagle making slow gyres far above. Castelo de Bode is a wonderful place, and the water is warm for much of the year. "Perfect", wrote our inspector.

**Rooms:** 2 with bath & wc, plus suite; also self-catering house.
**Price:** Double/Twin Esc 13,500-14,500; Suite (2-people) Esc 16,000-17,000; house Esc 22,000 per day; extra bed Esc 2,500.
**Breakfast:** Included.
**Meals:** None available.
**Closed:** Never.

From Tomar or Lisbon follow signs to Castelo de Bode. Keep straight on for 6km and follow signs for Quinta do Troviscal/Turismo Rural; after 2km there is another sign pointing to a track to the right. Follow track to Quinta.

# Quinta do Coalhos

Pego
2205-306 Coalhos-Abrantes
Ribatejo

**Tel:** 241 833294 / 833609
**Fax:** 241 833678
**E-mail:** rdc3389@mail.telepac.pt

**Isabel Alberty**

The Quinta do Coalhos, a confection of statuary, patterned roofs and fantastic decoration, was built in 1903 by a cousin of the current owner's grandfather for summer parties. The house, white and pale blue and set far away from the road, is Art Nouveau with oval windows, griffins on plinths and angels on columns. It is surrounded by trees, farmland and whispering canes near the River Tagus. Today it is a family home, and Isabel, a nurse, and company director José will soon make you feel part of their lively family. Across the cobbled courtyard, near a mock castle with battlements, is an equally fanciful but separate house converted into a rustic-style two-bedroom apartment. It has its own kitchen, a large fireplace, a private terrace at the back overlooking cane plantations, and a beautifully finished bathroom. Here you can be on your own or cross the courtyard to spend time with the family; Isabel may show you her collection of Portuguese furniture and ceramics. The fleur-de-lys-shaped swimming pool is girt with statues; there are also plenty of trees, and shaded tables and chairs. The house may be fantastically ornate but the atmosphere is friendly and down to earth.

**Rooms:** 2-bedroom apartment.
**Price:** Esc 14,000; Apartment Esc 17,500-20,000 (min. 2 nights).
**Breakfast:** Self-catering or included.
**Meals:** Available by arrangement.
**Closed:** August.

Leave the A1 motorway at Torres Novas, join the IP6 for Abrantes, cross Abrantes, cross the river, and turn left for Pego. Drive along for 4km, and look for the gates in a yellow wall on the left. Ring the bell and the gate will open.

**Map no: 4**

Entry no: 102

# Southern Portugal

Alentejo não tem sombra
Senão a que vem do ceu.
Abrigue se aqui, menina
Debaixo do meu chapeu.

The Alentejo has no shade
Save that which falls from above.
Take shelter here, maiden
Beneath the brim of my hat.
(Folk song)

## Quinta da Bela Vista
7320-014 Póvoa e Meadas
Alentejo

**Tel:** 245 968125
**Fax:** 245 968132
**E-mail:** jlporfirio@clix.pt
**Web:** www.eespe.com/belavista

**Maria Teresa Monteiro dos Santos**

The gently undulating hills planted with cork and olive, the long vistas and sense of space of this part of Portugal seem to make a visit here more than just a holiday; it touches you on a deeper level. The Quinta da Bela Vista is at the edge of a tiny Alentejo village, and Dona Maria's family have been here since the 1920s, when an uncle built the nearby dam. This is a family home, where books, magazines, photos, piano and card-table create a mood of intimacy while vast reception rooms, chandeliers and a busy maid evoke one of privilege. Of the bedrooms we best liked *Rosa* (no numbers here, insists Maria), which is decorated in a white-on-pink print of flying ducks and has a veranda with a view and a period bathroom. All bedrooms are large, have wooden floors and are really quiet; most have views out to nearby Castelo de Vide. Rather like staying with a favourite aunt, you enjoy family recipes (much of the meat is from the farm) and the quinta's own wine and *aguardente* (grape liqueur) and fresh eggs. A good place for a family stay; food and drink are always available and children will enjoy the huge games room, while outside there is a pool, tennis court, bicycles and horses.

**Rooms:** 4 with bath or shower & wc and 2 houses.
**Price:** Double/Twin Esc 15,000; House (for 2) Esc 12,000, (for 4) Esc 25,000, (for 6) Esc 33,000.
**Breakfast:** included.
**Meals:** Lunch/Dinner Esc 4,000; snacks also available.
**Closed:** January 5-20.

From Lisbon on N46 before Castelo de Vide take signposted turn for Póvoa e Meadas. Follow 'Turismo Rural' signs towards Póvoa then the signs for Quinta da Bela Vista.

**Map no: 4**

Entry no: 103

# Albergaria El Rei Dom Miguel

Rua Bartolomeu Alvares da Santa, Nº 45     **Tel:** 245 919191/90
7320 Castelo de Vide                    **Fax:** 245 901592
Alentejo

### Maria Vitoria Ribeiro Chamiço Heitor

Castelo de Vide is one of the Alentejo's most memorable hilltop villages; within
the town walls built by Dom Afonso in the 13th century, the old Jewish quarter
(you can visit the synagogue) climbs anarchically up towards the castle. Just to one
side of the lower town's main square this fine old town house has recently been
refurbished to create a small B&B. A granite staircase leads to the first floor and
the living quarters. Perhaps the house's most salient feature is its polished wooden
flooring in guest and public rooms. The many antiques in the lounge and corridors
give away Dona Maria Ribeiro's passion for period furniture. We particularly liked
the quiet drawing room with its old oratorio and figure of São Domingo and open
hearth (there is always a fire in the colder months). Bedrooms are more modern;
all of their wooden beds, writing and bedside tables are new, as are curtains and
bedspreads in matching (local) fabric. Special wall insulation and double glazing
guarantee a warm, peaceful night and the whole of the house is spic and span.
Excellent value at any time of the year and there's a cheerful little restaurant just
yards away.

**Rooms:** 7 with bath & wc.
**Price:** Twin Esc 8,000-12,000.
**Breakfast:** Included.
**Meals:** None available.
**Closed:** Never.

From Portalegre towards Marvão on E802,
then left on E246 to Castelo de Vide. At
main square of town, turn left onto main
street (known as 'carreira de cima'); hotel
on left.

Entry no: 104                                               Map no: 4

## Casa do Parque

Avenida da Aramenha 37
7320 Castelo de Vide
Alentejo

**Tel:** 245 901250
**Fax:** 245 901228

**Victor Guimarães**

In a beautiful backwater of the Alentejo, surrounded by stands of chestnut and acacia, the hilltop village of Castelo de Vide is girt around with its 13th-century town wall. Steep cobblestone alleys run up the hill through the old Jewish *call* to the Castle; make sure to visit the spring whose waters are said to cure everything. The focal point of the lower town is the leafy Praça Dom Pedro V and tucked away at one end of it you will find the gaily canopied Casa do Parque. The family are proud of their *hospitalidade portuguesa*; the feeling of homeliness spills over into the prettily-furnished guest rooms. They are surprisingly well-furnished (even though bathrooms are smallish) and are spotlessly clean; they have attractive wooden furniture and the mattresses lead you gently into the arms of Morpheus. In winter, hot-air heating warms the room in minutes. Don't miss dinner in the restaurant downstairs and the *migas alentejanas*, or one of the roast dishes; the dining room is a large, functional affair where you may be the only foreigner among local diners. Guests can enjoy a pool a kilometre away, at the owners' Casa dos Lilazes, which also has 10 rooms.

**Rooms:** 25 with bath & wc; 1 suite.
**Price:** Double/Twin Esc 6,500-10,000; Suite Esc 11,500.
**Breakfast:** Included.
**Meals:** Lunch/Dinner Esc 2,000-4,500.
**Closed:** Never.

From Portalegre towards Marvão on E802, then left on E246 to Castelo de Vide. Here into centre then right along the top of the park; hotel at end on left.

**Map no: 4**

Entry no: 105

# Casa de Borba

Rua da Cruz, Nº5                **Tel:** 268 894528
7150-125 Borba               **Fax:** 268 841448
Alentejo

**Maria José Tavares Lobo de Vasconcelos**

A gem of a house, it was built by Madame's forebears at the end of the 17th century; the surrounding estate is given over to olives, vineyards and livestock. The building earns a mention in the *inventário artístico de Portugal*; once you pass through the main entrance, an extraordinary neo-classical staircase leads you to the first floor living quarters. And what bedrooms await you here! They have high, delicately moulded ceilings, parquet floors softened by Arraiolos rugs, and are crammed with the family antiques. The *Bishop's room* (where the Archbishop of Évora stayed) has an 18th-century canopied bed; *Grandmother's room* has an unusual lift-up sink; there are baths with feet, old prints, and long curtains in front of the windows looking over a delectable garden. The lounge and breakfast room are similarly elegant; breakfast arrives via the 'dumb waiter'. Your hosts are quiet, refined folk and they skimp on nothing to please you; at night, hot water is delivered to your room together with cake and a selection of teas. During the day choose between the long covered gallery, a corner of the walled garden or the billiards room. A house of beauty and tranquillity.

**Rooms:** 5 with bath & wc.
**Price:** Double/Twin Esc 15,000.
**Breakfast:** Included.
**Meals:** None available.
**Closed:** December 20-28.

From Estremoz N4 to Borba. Casa de Borba is in town centre close to Correios (post office).

Entry no: 106                                              Map no: 4

# Casa de Peixinhos
7160 Vila Viçosa
Alentejo

**Tel:** 268 980472/980859
**Fax:** 268 881348

**José Passanha**

Casa de Peixinhos is, like vintage port, a rich, mellow experience, the fruit of time and patience. Once you pass under the main portal and into the cobbled courtyard, the main façade has a distinctly exotic feel; its arches and triple turrets are softened by whitewashed walls with broad bands of ochre. Inside the main building the mood is more classical; this is a superbly maintained aristocratic house and, though much of the décor and furnishing is period, everything sparkles freshly. The sitting room is a handsome introduction to the house, with mouldings, a leather three-piece and the family coat of arms above the hearth. Leading off it is the dining room, the mouldings enhanced with gold drapes, chandeliers and beautifully arranged flowers. This is the sort of place where you might dress for the traditional Alentejo cooking. Rooms are among the loveliest we have come across in Portugal, some decorated in blues, others in *sang de boeuf*, and each one different. One has *Dona Maria* beds, another canopied twins; all of them have gorgeous bathrooms with locally quarried marble. A regal house.

**Rooms:** 7 with bath & wc; 1 suite.
**Price:** Double/Twin Esc 17,500; Single Esc 14,000; Suite Esc 23,000; extra bed Esc 3,500.
**Breakfast:** Included.
**Meals:** On request, Lunch/Dinner from Esc 4,000.
**Closed:** Never.

From Évora to Vila Viçosa. Here follow signs towards Borba into Vila V. town centre. Just past the Mercado Municipal, turn right and follow signs.

**Map no: 4**                                                        Entry no: 107

# Herdade do Monte Branco

Rio de Moinhos
7150 Borba
Alentejo

**Tel:** 21 483 0834/5
    96 630 1336/96 298 8099 (mob)
**Fax:** 21 486 3403
**E-mail:** montebranco@netcabo.pt
**Web:** pwp.netcabo.pt/0218645001

**The Medeiros family**

Few places can be more tranquil than this estate on the sunny flanks of a hillside near Borba, a region famous for its wine and cork. The Herdade is well off the beaten track, a restored farmhouse and outbuildings which have been converted into apartments by one of the owners, architect José Calado. It has been beautifully furnished in typical Alentejo style, with old furniture, much of it hand-painted in the Alentejo floral style. The tiles in the bathrooms and kitchens have also been painted by José's wife, artist Maria João. Your hosts are friendly, educated people who readily share their enthusiasm for this region. The bedrooms are countryfied and simple, with whitewashed walls, exposed beams, tile floors and comfortable beds. You will awake to the sounds of birds and rustling trees. There is a large rustic games room/bar and restaurant, and the food is excellent. The Herdade is near cork trees and forest, and beside having its own pool, it is only a short walk to a lake hidden in the trees. Other diversions include cork, wine and cheese production, and clay pigeon shooting. You can also go on nature tours or be taken to prehistoric sites in the area. Ideal for nature-lovers and families.

**Rooms:** 9 1, 2 and 4-bed apartments, sleeping 2-8.
**Price:** From Esc 9,000 per room/night.
**Breakfast:** Included.
**Meals:** Lunch/Dinner on request, Esc 3,500, plus self-catering.
**Closed:** Never.

On the A2 from Lisbon, southbound, take the A6 eastbound, and exit at Estremoz and join the N4. Look for signs to Gloria and then for Rio de Moinhos. Monte Branco is signposted to the right.

Entry no: 108

Map no: 4

# Quinta da Talha

Estrada do Freixo
7170 Redondo
Alentejo

**Tel:** 266 999468
**Fax:** 21 386 4224

**Manuel António Mantero Morães**

This archetypal Alentejo farmhouse, with windows and doors highlighted with broad bands of blue, is 2km from Redondo, and the vines which surround the house go to make the superb red wine of the same name. A delightful family home, you may meet Senhor Manuel; this genteel and friendly soul will regale you with the history of family and farm and has a fondness for England born of his wife's Anglo-Saxon lineage. See the photos of their ancestors and 11 grandchildren in the Quinta's lounge; under arched ceilings it is elegant, full of treasured family antiques. There are comfy blue and white striped sofas, Queen Anne chairs, a photo of the last Queen of Portugal and a framed Papal dispensation allowing Mass to be celebrated next door. The dining room is just as quietly elegant. Rooms and apartments are in the farm's converted outbuildings. They are more rustic in tone, and very pleasing with unusual paper-cut *bentinhos* above the beds from the Redondo Convent, old metal bedsteads and woodburners, and striped prints on bedspreads and curtains. Outside enjoy walking, groves of fruit trees, a swing and sand pit, flattish terrain for biking and the old water tank for swimming.

**Rooms:** 3 with bath & wc; 1 apartment.
**Price:** Twin Esc 11,000; Apt Esc 22,000.
**Breakfast:** Included.
**Meals:** None available.
**Closed:** Christmas.

From Évora take 254 to Redondo then 524 to Freixo. After 2.5km Quinta signposted to right.

# Hotel Convento de São Paulo

Aldeia da Serra
7170-120 Redondo
Alentejo

**Tel:** 266 989160
**Fax:** 266 999104
**E-mail:** hotelconvspaulo@mail.telepac.pt
**Web:** www.hotel-convento-de-Sao-Paulo.p

**Maria Júlia Leotte**

Superb in all respects, this massive monastery was built by Paulist monks who came to the D'Ossa mountain slopes in the 12th century. For 500 years they embellished their place of worship and imbued it with an atmosphere of spirituality and calm: today, as you pass through the enormous old door your voice may instinctively drop. See the 54,000 hand-painted tiles that decorate chapel, corridors and gardens, the largest collection in Europe. A red carpet softens terracotta floors and sweeps you along to the rooms, each occupying two cells, their uncluttered feel in keeping with São Paulo's past, and bathrooms with brass taps and white marble. Public areas, too, live up to expectations, for there are some lovely 'pieces', many of them Leotte family heirlooms (owners for the last 130 years). Under vaulted ceilings the dining room is cosy, the lounge has well-dressed sofas; eclectic modern art lends a lighter note plus there are a games room and cloisters. Outside enjoy the beautiful tiled patio depicting the four seasons, a swimming pool under trees, wonderful views and walks through wooded slopes of the 600-hectare estate which provides fruit, vegetables and meat. The spirit soars.

**Rooms:** 29 with bath & wc.
**Price:** Single Esc 17,000-31,000; Double/Twin Esc 22,000-43.000 (Extra bed Esc 9,500).
**Breakfast:** Included, in Restaurant 'O Ermita'.
**Meals:** Lunch/Dinner approx. Esc 5,500.
**Closed:** Never.

From Lisbon towards Madrid on motorway. Exit for Estremoz, then direction of Elvas for about 5km then towards Redondo. The hotel is 15km on.

# Albergaria Solar de Monfalim

Largo da Misericórdia No. 1
7000-646 Évora
Alentejo

**Tel:** 266 750000
**Fax:** 266 742367
**E-mail:** reservas@monfalimtur.pt
**Web:** www.monfalimtur.pt

**Ana Ramalho Serrabulho**

Monfalim is Évora's oldest hostelry and received its first paying guest in 1892, though its history goes back to the mid-16th century. It is at the heart of beautiful old Évora on a cobbled square where huge jacaranda trees soften the urban contours; the façade is a treat with its elegant first floor arcade built over the former stables. Pass beneath the coat of arms, climb the heavy granite staircase and emerge to meet the smartly uniformed reception staff – all to the strains of piped muzak. But fear not, this is a truly friendly hostelry and you are made to feel a valued guest at all times. Perhaps miss the lounge/TV room and choose instead a delightful little bar where old photos tell tales of the Alentejo's rural life. The dining room is large, light and leads out to the first floor, arcaded terrace where you can linger over your (buffet) breakfast. And what perfect rooms! They are high-ceilinged with old wrought iron and brass bedsteads, lovely cotton sheets and bedspreads; old lamps, tiled floors and Arraiolos rugs together add up to our type of bedroom idyll. Best time to visit? It has to be May or June when those jacarandas bring forth their glorious purple.

**Rooms:** 25 with bath or shower & wc;
1 suite.
**Price:** Double/Twin Esc 12,000-14,500;
Suite Esc 13,000-16,000.
**Breakfast:** Included.
**Meals:** none available.
**Closed:** Never.

On arriving in Évora follow green tourist signs which indicate where the hotels are; in detail: look for exit off from ring road up Rua de Machede via Portas de Moura into Rua Miguel Bombarda; turn right into Largo da Misericórdia.

**Map no: 4**                                              Entry no: 111

# Casa de Sam Pedro

Quinta de Sam Pedro
7000-173 Évora
Alentejo

**Tel:** 266 707731
   96 236 2050 (mob)
**Fax:** 266 744859

**Antonio Pestana de Vasconcellos**

A delectable address, close to wonderful Évora and utterly bucolic. A sense of well-being takes hold as soon as you turn off the narrow country road and follow a winding track through old olive groves. The house offers a benevolent greeting; acacias throw shade across its uncluttered façade and the air is filled with birdsong. Inside, the decoration is gentle, unshowy: a grandfather clock, parquet floors set against old *azulejos*, gilt mirrors and the family china. The dining room is elegant but cosy, the kitchen as a great kitchen can be, the real heart of the house. We could imagine snuggling down with a good book on one of the sofas in front of the white-tiled hearth, beneath the collection of old plates and copper saucepans. (We would also choose to breakfast here – tell your host if you feel the same.) The peace of the place makes you more aware of those gently creaking floorboards as you climb to your room. Here the decoration is again subdued and utterly 'family'; perhaps a *Mater Dolorosa* above a bed, a lovely old antique wardrobe, or a fine old dressing table. Wholly authentic – this is the type of rural tourism we admire.

**Rooms:** 3 with bath & wc.
**Price:** Double Esc 12,500;
Twin Esc 12,500.
**Breakfast:** Included.
**Meals:** None available.
**Closed:** 15-30 August & 15-30 December.

From Évora take Estremoz road, but immediately left at roundabout towards Igrejinha. Continue, then left at fork towards Sr. dos Aflitos. After approx. 2.5km, entrance on left to Sam Pedro. Keep left on track.

# Quinta da Espada

Apartado 68
Estrada de Arraiolos Km 4
7002-501 Évora
Alentejo

**Tel:** 266 734549
**Fax:** 266 736464
**E-mail:** quintadaespada@clix.pt

**Maria Isabel Sousa Cabral**

Quinta da Espada ('of the sword'; the one hidden here by no less a man than Geraldo Geraldes, he who snatched Évora back from the Moors), surrounded by groves of olives and cork oaks and with views down to Évora, is a low, whitewashed, mimosa-graced building with ochre window surrounds and a perfectly authentic atmosphere. Bedrooms vary in size and colour scheme, with the delicately hand-painted Alentejo furniture everywhere; terracotta tiles, *estera* matting and dark beams creating a rustic mood. Little touches, like towels with a hand-embroidered 'Quinta da Espada' motif, add a touch of gentility to it all. Slate is an unusual and attractive alternative in the bathrooms. The Green room occupies what was once the (small) family chapel. We particularly liked the smaller sitting room where you breakfast and dine in front of the hearth during the colder months. You may well be tempted by the Alentejo cooking, but if not you can make use of a well-equipped guest kitchen. Do stay two nights and walk into Évora along tracks that lead out from the Quinta, or ramble out and explore the 12-hectare estate. Or float about in its swimming pool, perfect in hotter weather.

**Rooms:** 6 with bath & wc; 1 suite.
**Price:** Double/Twin Esc 13,500; Single Esc 9500; Suite Esc 16,500.
**Breakfast:** Included.
**Meals:** Lunch/Dinner on request, Esc 4,000.
**Closed:** December 24-25.

From Évora take the road towards Arraiolos and after 4km Quinta is signposted to right.

## Pensão Policarpo

Rua da Freiria de Baixo, 16
7000-898 Évora
Alentejo

**Tel:** 266 702424
**Fax:** 266 702424
**Web:** www.localnet.pt/residencialpolicarpo

**Michèle Policarpo**

This grand town mansion was built by the Counts of Lousã in the 16th century, only to be lost to the State during the purges of Pombal. It was abandoned, but then rescued some 60 years ago by the Policarpo family. They carefully set about restoration and created the most intimate of guesthouses and all these years on still have buckets of enthusiasm for their work. The breakfast room is a delight; it has a high, vaulted ceiling and the three enormous windows capture the morning sunlight. *Fado* at breakfast takes your meal into another dimension; outside is a terrace where you can eat *al fresco* on warmer days. There is a cosy sitting room (in what once was the kitchen) with hand-painted tiles, and a part of the old town wall has been swallowed up within the house as Évora grew outwards. Bedrooms are reached via the original granite staircase. Some have vaulted ceilings, many have pretty hand-painted Alentejo furniture and a number have antique bits and bobs. Our favourite was 101, with its original tiles and inspirational view. A private car park is a big plus in a town of narrow streets and traffic wardens. *Note that the entrance to the car park is in Rua Conde da Serra.*

**Rooms:** 12 with bath or shower & wc;
8 sharing bath & wc.
**Price:** Double/Twin Esc 13,000;
Apartment Esc 20,000.
**Breakfast:** Included.
**Meals:** None available.
**Closed:** Never.

Arriving in Évora from Lisbon, follow ring road round city until you see signs for Policarpo (close to University). Hotel has free car park under archway.

# Monte da Serralheira

Estrada de Bairro de Almeirim          **Tel:** 266 741286/743957
7000-788 Évora                         **Fax:** 266 741286
Alentejo

**George & Lucia van der Feltz**

George and Lucia discovered the wide, open spaces of the Alentejo more than 20 years ago and here they are now, farming the land just outside historic Évora and well integrated into the local community. They are still as enthralled by this wonderful country as they were in their pioneering days. Their generosity is reflected in the size and design of the apartments that occupy what once were the workers' quarters. They have their own terraces, four of them have woodburning stoves and all are high-ceilinged. They have all you need if self-catering. This could be the ideal place for a longer (family) stay. Leave guide books behind and let yourself be led by Lucia; she is a professional guide and has a number of well-documented 'circuits' out from Serralheira. And if birds are your thing, stay here; George is an expert. You'll hear nightingales if here on a spring night. Horses and an instructor are available, and there's a games room. This isolated 200-year-old farmhouse, with its large garden and terraces, exuberant bougainvillaea and wisteria, whitewashed walls offset by blue trimmings and splendidly isolated setting is a most 'special' place in the rural peace of the southern plains.

**Rooms:** 1, 2 & 3 bed apartments sleeping 2-6 with shower & wc.
**Price:** Double/Twin Esc 13,000; Apartment Esc 20,000.
**Breakfast:** Esc 950 (if not self-catering).
**Meals:** None available.
**Closed:** Never.

From Lisbon to Évora. There right onto ring road. Right at roundabout next to Opel garage towards Almeirim (sul). Follow this road to very end to the farm.

**Map no: 4**                                              Entry no: 115

# Monte Cabeça do Ouro

7570 Grândola  
Alentejo

**Tel:** 269 451292  
**Fax:** 269 441053  
**E-mail:** ant.menezes@clix.pt

**António Menezes e Cunha**

In a wonderful position high on a ridge, this Alentejo farmhouse looks out to hillsides cloaked in cork, olive and pine trees and to the old town of Grândola which is mentioned in the famous song which signalled the beginning the bloodless revolution of 1974. Cabeça do Ouro is a working farm: you'll see horses, pigs, goats, sheep and duck. There are any number of activities to choose from: you can ride, take a jeep excursion, go canoeing, sail on the Sado estuary or take a boat from the coast, just 15km away, to see flamingo and dolphins. Guest rooms are in regional style with terracotta floors, simple iron beds and traditional patterned blankets – and the bathrooms are attractive, too. The self-catering cottages or *Montes* are large, with fireplaces in their living rooms. The big communal breakfast area has tables and bentwood chairs on an upper level, and long white sofas and a big fireplace down below – a good place to relax in company. At meal times, if you're not self-catering, expect plenty of pork or head out to one of the local restaurants which specialise in fish and shellfish. There's also a barbecue by the pool, and a bread oven.

**Rooms:** 12 with bath & wc; 3 cottages.  
**Price:** Double/Twin Esc 10,000-15,000; Single Esc 9,000-14,500; cottage (for 4) Esc 20,000-28,000 (2/3 nights min. stay.)  
**Breakfast:** Included in rooms; house self-catering.  
**Meals:** Dinner Esc 3,700, by arrangement.  
**Closed:** Never.

Take the road from Grândola to Santiago do Caçem and after 3km there is a sign to Agroturismo to left. Go up the hill to house.

## Casa Santos Murteira

Rua de S. Pedro 68/70/72
7090 Alcáçovas
Alentejo

**Tel:** 266 954744
**Fax:** 266 954105

**Maria da Encarnação Fernandes**

This old village house was just too good not to share. The main façade captures the eye with its exquisite wrought-iron balconies and Baroque flourish above the cornicing; at its midst a guardian angel stands sentinel. The style within could be described as 'unpretentiously elegant'; the lounge is a gem with its polished parquet floor, comfy chairs, chandelier and collection of books and oils. The Virgin and Christ child look on from above the hearth. The cream and mustard dining room is just as special; light floods in from shuttered windows on two sides and there is a beautiful Arraiolos rug beneath a Queen Ann-ish dining table. Just outside is a terrace for al fresco meals when it is warm. The back of the house has a more Alentejano feel with its terracotta tiles, wafer bricking and bands of blue highlighting windows and doors. A spring-fed pool sits prettily in an orange grove. There are just six bedrooms and they are among the nicest we know; fine old beds, marble-topped bedside tables, planked and rugged floors and splendidly moulded ceilings. The housekeeper does her best to make your stay memorable.

**Rooms:** 6 with bath & wc.
**Price:** Double/Twin Esc 14,000.
**Breakfast:** Included.
**Meals:** Dinner occasionally on request.
**Closed:** Never.

From Évora take ring road round town until Alcáçovas signposted. There, Rua de S. Pedro runs parallel to main street; house halfway up on the left.

**Map no: 5**

Entry no: 117

# Monte do Sobral

Estrada Alcáçovas-Viana
7090 Alcáçovas
Alentejo

**Tel:** 266 954717
**Fax:** 266 954105

**Marco Fragoso Fernandes**

Splendidly isolated and surrounded by its 300-hectare estate, Monte do Sobral is every inch the classic Alentejo farmstead: blue and white, Roman tiled, long, low and broad-chimneyed. Most of the apartments occupy the old stable block; all have old floor tiles, a hearth, low-beamed ceilings and a small sitting room. A couple of them have a wooden mezzanine which children would love them. A flock of bird prints, antlers above the hearths and animal skins on the floor reflect the owner's love of the hunt. Each of the smallish apartments has a small fridge – a useful extra in the fierce summer months. Across the way in the main farmhouse there is an unusual guest lounge; this too is a mezzanine affair with a small bar in one corner. Do dine in at least once on the traditional country food prepared by Sobral's cheery housekeeper; it is remarkably good value. Otherwise, Alcáçovas is just a short drive away. If you tire of the pool and its long views out across the beautiful open countryside, there are horses to ride – even a cart that can be harnessed up – mountain biking and walks across the estate. Particularly good for family holidays.

**Rooms:** 6 apartments.
**Price:** Esc 6,000 per person.
**Breakfast:** Included.
**Meals:** Dinner Esc 3,000 on request.
**Closed:** Never.

From Montemor towards Évora then right towards Viana. Monte do Sobral signposted to right.

Entry no: 118        Map no: 4

# Casa de Terena

Rua Direita, 45
7250-065 Terena-Alandroal
Alentejo

**Tel:** 268 459132
**Fax:** 268 459155
**E-mail:** casadeterena@mail.telepac.pt

**António & Conceição Pimenta de Castro**

Terena is a pretty and unspoilt (and virtually undiscovered) village; if you approach from, the north, all you see at first is the medieval castle; the village has developed on the hill's south-western slopes in typical whitewashed Altentejo style. Groups of village ladies were sunning themselves, bent over their lace, the day that we visited and we could see why Conchita and António were inspired to move here from Lisbon. It was a labour of love to nurse this grand old 18th-century village house back to life. From the inner dragon-tooth patio a grand marble staircase sweeps you up to the bedrooms. Here you'll find wrought-iron bedsteads (with new mattresses), Alentejo rugs, terracotta tiles, dried flowers and views out to the reservoir beyond – and all sparkling like new. And there are Casablanca-style ceiling fans to cool things down when the heat sets in. The downstairs sitting room has wafer-bricked, vaulted ceilings, a large fireplace red and blue armchairs and dark red velvet curtains; it's a good room for *tertulias*, late-night talks. The tranquillity and beauty of Terena and your hosts' enthusiasm make the journey worthwhile. Abundant bird life for ornithologists.

**Rooms:** 6 with bath & wc.
**Price:** Single Esc 10,000; Double/Twin Esc 12,000.
**Breakfast:** Included – buffet.
**Meals:** Lunch/Dinner Esc 3,500.
**Closed:** Never.

Coming from Spain through Badajoz and on into Portugal towards Évora. Terena is half way between Vila Viçosa and Monsaraz. House next to castle.

**Map no: 4**            Entry no: 119

# Horta da Moura

Hotel Rural
Monsaraz – apartado 64
7200-999 Reguengos de Monsaraz
Alentejo

**Tel:** 266 550100
**Fax:** 266 550108
**E-mail:** hortadamoura@hotmail.com
**Web:** www.hortadamoura.pt

**Ludovina Calado**

Monsaraz is one of the treasures of the Alentejo, an ancient hilltop fortress village
of cobbled streets and whitewashed walls, visible for miles and with near-circular
views from its battlements of the Alentejo plains. On the slopes below lies the
Horta da Moura estate, whose name recalls the Moorish invaders of the eighth
century. It is a modern extension of an old house, but regional character is
everywhere, with exposed stone and local slate, tiled floors strewn with rugs, and
arched brick ceilings (typical of the Moors) or rustic wooden beams. Both suites
and rooms are of a good size, with working fireplaces, arched ceilings and dark
wood furniture. It feels immensely solid, and stout walls keep you cool indoors in
the hottest weather. Do try the regional restaurant's local meat and fish, the
superb local wines, as well as vegetarian food from the Swiss chef. The circular
Torreão bar has a rooftop terrace where you can take the air. Here you can
experience the Alentejo lifestyle, many added pleasures, including the games room
for table tennis and the pool. If you fancy an excursion there are horses to ride (10
plus a pony), an elegant horse-drawn carriage and bicycles.

**Rooms:** 6 rooms, 13 junior and 6 senior
suites, plus 1 2-bedroom suite, all with
bath & wc.
**Price:** Double Esc 16,000-20,000; Suite
Esc 20,000-25,000.
**Breakfast:** Included.
**Meals:** Lunch/Dinner Esc 4,000.
**Closed:** Never.

Follow directions to Monsaraz, and when
just below the fortress walls, instead of
turning right, follow the road to Mourão. The estate is well signposted.

# Monte Alerta

Apartado 101
7200 Monsaraz
Alentejo

**Tel:** 266 550150
**Fax:** 266 557325
**E-mail:** montealerta@mail.telepac.pt
**Web:** www.montealerta.co.pt

**Sergio Ambrosio**

In the garden you see Spain in one direction and the famous hilltop town of Monsaraz in the other. Monte Alerta is a classic Alentejo farmhouse, white with blue borders to doors and windows, tall chimneys and terracotta roofs. The old farmhouse, which sits so well in this landscape of red earth, cork trees and heat haze, has been professionally overhauled in recent years, so everything is clean, new and very well cared for by friendly housekeeper Joaquina. Behind the thick walls the bedrooms are remarkably large, and the air-conditioning will be welcome in high summer. Polished tile floors are strewn with rugs and there are good quality covers on the beds; the choice of colours is excellent. Some beds have wooden headboards, others wrought-iron, such as room 4 with its views of Monsaraz and the old convent. The bathrooms are enormous, as are the dining room, with its long table and rustic chairs, and games room, the latter with big leather sofas, pool table and woodburner. There are lots of typical Alentejo touches here, in the brick arches and arched *abodoba* ceilings. The walls are hung with hunting and floral prints, an old 19th-century sampler and religious subjects.

**Rooms:** 8 with bath & wc; 1 suite for 4 people.
**Price:** Double/Twin Esc 15,000; Single Esc 12,000; Suite Esc 20,000; extra bed Esc 3,000.
**Breakfast:** Included.
**Meals:** For groups of eight or more.
**Closed:** Never.

From Évora to Reguengos, then follow signs to S. Pedro do Corval; continue to the village of Telheiro and look for signs to the house 800m away; it is easy to find.

**Map no: 6**

Entry no: 121

# Casa da Muralha

Rua das Portas de Beja, Nº 43
7830-431 Serpa
Alentejo

**Tel:** 284 54 31 50
**Fax:** 284 54 31 51

**Mário Trigo Cortez Pereira**

Against the city wall, and towered over by the ancient aqueduct, is the Casa da
Muralha, an elegant 17th-century townhouse furnished and decorated to
perfection. Stroll through otherworldly, narrow winding streets of this unspoilt,
whitewashed town to this family-owned house, which you enter through a cool,
vaulted, cobbled coach house. On a hot day the contrast between this welcome
shade and that of the courtyard garden, with the heat and brightness of the
surrounding plain, is welcome – this Beja region is always the hottest place in
Portugal in the summer. Three bedrooms in the main house are large and
traditional, with vaulted ceilings and good modern bathrooms; there are two more
at the bottom of the garden, new but decorated like the others with rustic painted
Alentejo furniture. All are comfortable and, when needed, air conditioned. The
dining room opens onto the garden and breakfast is usually served outside on the
cobbled terrace, where there are orange and palm trees. Owners Mário and Paula,
and their maid Claudia, are friendly and informative; Claudia may take you
through an upstairs kitchen window for a stroll on the city walls.

**Rooms:** 5 with bath/shower & wc.
**Price:** Double/Twin Esc 10,000;
Single Esc 8,000.
**Breakfast:** Included.
**Meals:** None available.
**Closed:** Never.

It is well signposted in Serpa; look for signs
to 'Turismo Rural'. The house is just inside
one of the ancient gates in the city wall, on
the Beja side.

Entry no: 122

**Map no: 6**

# Convento de São Francisco Mértola

7750 Mértola
Alentejo

**Tel:** 286 612119
**Fax:** 286 612541
(& answering machine)

### Geraldine Zwanikken

Art, nature, history and spirituality meet in a most unusual way in this former Franciscan monastery with 90 acres, overlooking the junction of the rivers Guardiana and Oeiras and the ancient city of Mértola. When Dutch artist Geraldine and her late husband bought the *convento* in 1980, it was in ruins. The church is now an art gallery with Geraldine's pictures on show. There are art studios for artists-in-residence and spaces for meditation and yoga, which Geraldine teaches. It's not 'posh' or grand, more arty and alternative. She says "It's not really a holiday place, more for people who want to go on retreat or do something such as paint or meditate. There's bird-watching, canoeing and riding too". Two bedrooms were once monks' cells and have large doubles, terracotta floors and views over the river; another larger one has its own terrace, plus there is a lovely rustic cottage and a dormitory. Breakfast is in the cosy kitchen at a big table, and meals are *'estilo convento'*, mostly vegetarian wholefood (there's an organic garden). There are many courtyards and places to sit in the garden from where you'll see storks and circling kestrels above.

**Rooms:** 1 with shower & wc; 2 sharing shower & wc. Dormitory, plus cottage and studios (for artists in residence) also available.
**Price:** Single Esc 5,000 (Full board Esc 7,250); dormitory Esc 3,000; cottage Esc 45,000 per week.
**Breakfast:** Included for rooms and dormitory. Cottage self-catering.
**Meals:** Dinner Esc 1,500, available on request.
**Closed:** Never.

Leaving Mértola in the direction of the Algarve on Route 122, you pass the old bridge over the River Oeiras; the Convento is on the left.

**Map no: 6**

Entry no: 123

# Herdade da Matinha

7555-231 Cercal do Alentejo
Alentejo

**Tel:** 269 949247
**Fax:** 269 949247
**E-mail:** info@herdadedamatinha.com
**Web:** www.herdadedamatinha.com

### Alfredo Moreira da Silva

This a classic Alentejo farmhouse; long, low and encircled by the striking russet-brown trunks of the cork oak. Yet though the setting is deeply rural you are close to the wonders of the Alentejo's protected Costa Vicentina and to the towns of Cercal and Vila Nova de Milfontes. Monica works part of the year as a tourist guide and will help plan your sorties; Alfredo is an artist and looks after the cooking. He loves to chat with guests in the kitchen while preparing meals, probably to classical or baroque music. His paintings add life and colour to the lounge which is large, light and comfortable and leads to a terrace where camellias give way to groves of citrus – a lovely spot for meals when it's warm. Centre stage at Matinha is the kitchen and a big wooden table where you eat breakfast *en famille* and where dinner promises "the best traditional dishes but healthier than usual" (i.e. with more and better-prepared vegetables). Bedrooms are large, uncluttered, slate-floored and home to more of Alfredo's paintings; furnishings seem rather Conran in inspiration. Come for the utter peace, an interesting mixture of 'trad' Portugal with modern elements, and to meet your polyglot hosts.

**Rooms:** 4 with shower & wc; 2 suites.
**Price:** Double/Twin Esc 12,500-15,000;
Suite Esc 12,500-15,000.
**Breakfast:** Included.
**Meals:** Dinner Esc 3,500.
**Closed:** Never.

From Lisbon A2 to Grandola then towards
Sines on IP8 then IC4 to Cercal then
N390 to Vila Nova de Milfontes. Here,
opposite Frezas factory right and follow
signs along 3km of track.

# Verdemar

Casas Novas
7555-026 Cercal do Alentejo
Alentejo

**Tel:** 269 904544
**Fax:** 269 904544
**E-mail:** verdemar.cercal@mail.telepac.pt
**Web:** www.verdemar.net

### Nuno Vilas-Boas & Christine Nijhoff

Although only a short drive from the Atlantic beaches, Verdemar's setting is bucolic. Hidden away among stands of old cork oaks beyond the blue and white main gate a very special country retreat awaits you. Guest rooms are spread around the outbuildings but the focus is the main farmhouse and dining room (see photo). The atmosphere is easy and cosy; a beam and tongue and groove ceiling, an open kitchen/bar, wooden stools and chairs. You'll share fun and good food around one big table – *al fresco*, of course, in summer. Nuno, a professional chef for 20 years in Amsterdam, loves to have your company as he prepares dinner and likes to exchange a recipe or two. Leading off the kitchen, the lounge is equally cosy – guitar, paintings, an old lamp; a cool place to escape summer heat. And it is heartening to find somewhere so ready to welcome families with young children; they'll meet ducks, chickens, donkeys, cows and sheep. A children's dinner is even prepared early evening. Bedrooms are just right; no hotel extras but nothing lacking. There is a very attractive swimming pool, too, fenced off for the safety of children. Our type of idyll – with the true spirit of honest hostelry.

**Rooms:** 5 with bath & wc; 3 cottages.
**Price:** Double/Twin Esc 9,000-15,000; Cottages Esc 9,000-16,400.
**Breakfast:** Included; apartments self-catering.
**Meals:** Dinner on request, Esc 3,200. Not on Sundays.
**Closed:** Never.

From Lisbon A2 then IP1 towards Algarve. 500m after Mimosa right towards Cercal; 7km before you arrive in Cercal left on track at sign for Casas Novas; house signposted.

**Map no: 5**

Entry no: 125

# The Studio

Cela Vermelha
Cela Nature Reserve
7555 Cercal do Alentejo
Alentejo

**Tel:** 269 949100

**Carol Dymond**

The Cela valley is a paradise in hills facing the Atlantic beaches. Cela Vermelha, in a 70-acre nature reserve, is isolated, and on clear nights you can see *all* the stars. Owner Carol is an artist and massage therapist who also looks after conservation volunteers, tackles environment issues, plants trees and makes paper. You stay in a sunny, self-catering apartment, once a studio, and as original as she is. The gallery bedroom is reached via a yacht-style ladder, and up there you find a comfortable double bed and two single mattresses. Below is the living/kitchen area, a blue and white theme which includes both local handicrafts and her own pictures. Guests can self-cater (you can see the sea as you make your own solar-powered pop-up toast) or choose Carol's wholesome wholefood cooking, which can include vegan and vegetarian meals. There's an organic garden where you can pick the oranges and salad vegetables in season, and beyond that, walks into the hills. Carol is friendly and enthusiastic about the region, and will direct you down to the year-round stream in which there's a small natural pool just for guests. Unspoilt beaches are 8km away. *Minimum 3 nights stay.*

**Rooms:** 1 with shower & wc.
**Price:** Double/Twin Esc 10,000;
Esc 65,000 per week.
**Breakfast:** Esc 750.
**Meals:** Lunch Esc 1,000; Dinner
Esc 2,500.
**Closed:** Never.

From Cercal take the road to Vila Nova do Milfontes; after 6km, just before a sharp bend to the right, left at signpost to 'Cela'.
You then have a 3km roller-coaster ride through the hills, with great views!

Entry no: 126

Map no: 5

# Castelo de Milfontes
7645 Vila Nova de Milfontes    **Tel:** 283 998231
Alentejo                       **Fax:** 283 997122

**Ema M. da Câmara Machado**

Carthaginians, Romans, Moors and even Algerian pirates have coveted the remarkable strategic site now held by the Castelo de Milfontes; you see why when looking out across the river estuary to the Atlantic beyond. The fort dates from the 16th century and was rescued from ruin by the family 50 years ago. This is no ordinary 'hotel' and the spirit of welcome is captured in the plaque above the hearth: *'viver sem amigos não é viver'* (living without friends is not living). Half-board is the thing at Milfontes and dinner the occasion to meet your fellow guests and Ema, who graciously officiates at table. It is an occasion to dress for; at 8 o'clock a maid announces it is time to pass through to the dining room – silver service and traditional Portuguese food await you. The rooms have views that defy description; we think tower room 1 is one of the loveliest we have seen anywhere. The furniture matches the castle; perhaps an old writing desk, a baldequin bed, original oils – and all poised between vaulted ceilings and parquet floors. The Castelo's fame has spread far and wide and guests return year after year; spend a night here and you will never forget it. *Half-board only.*

**Rooms:** 7 with bath & wc.
**Price:** Single Esc 20,500; Double/Twin Esc 28,700 (half-board for two). Tower rooms: Single 21,600; Double 30,900 (half-board).
**Breakfast:** Included.
**Meals:** Picnic Lunches Esc 2,700; Dinner included in price.
**Closed:** Never.

From Lisbon, A2 to Setúbal, then N10 towards Évora and branch right on N5/N20 toward Grandola. Left on N120 to Santiago and on to Cercal. Here, N390 to V.N. de Milfontes. Castle at edge of estuary by beach.

**Map no: 5**                                    Entry no: 127

# Casa do Pinhal/Casa da Vinha

Cova da Zorra
São Luis
7630 Odemira
Alentejo

**Tel:** 283 998443
**Fax:** 283 998510
**E-mail:** at5@mail.telepac.pt

### Teresa Beirão & Alexandre Bastos

Pines, cork trees and vines surround these two typical Alentejano houses, which are light, airy and simple, with some lovely touches. Alexandre and Teresa are both architects who specialise in *taipa* (rammed earth) buildings, the traditional building method in this area, and they have inspired a revival of interest in it. Their hallmark is to leave large areas of the *taipa* visible, revealing the construction method; otherwise the walls are white. Alexandre is also a painter his pictures hang in both houses. Floors are pale terracotta tiles, furniture is simple, and there is a fireplace in Pinhal and a woodburner in Vinha. Bedrooms are simple and very restful, a pleasant blend of old and new, and bathrooms are decorated with modern *azulejos*. The houses have a common door, so can be let as one for larger groups. They are sited just outside the village and have open views below; you can relax outside or take the air up on the roof terrace. From here you will see the pines and vineyards. Your hosts make their own wine and if you're there in September you might be invited to help gather and tread the grapes.

**Rooms:** 2 two-bed self-catering houses.
**Price:** Double/Twin Esc 10,000,
Esc 70,000 per week; extra bed Esc 1000.
**Breakfast:** Self-catering.
**Meals:** Self-catering.
**Closed:** Never.

As you enter S. Luis (midway between Odemira and Cercal), turn at signpost to Bairro Azul, Cova da Zorra and Garatuja. After 600m, near a long building, turn right, and then right again, up the hill, to the houses. Host usually meets guests to show them the way.

# Cortinhas

Vale Bejinha
2581 Cx. S. Luis
7632 Odemira
Alentejo

**Tel:** 283 976076
**E-mail:** walkdontwalk80@hotmail.com

### Sophie & Tuke Taylor

"I try to make it look as though someone lives here," says Sophie, so this is no soulless holiday cottage. You arrive at the back and it looks like a simple, tiny old house in ochre limewash. Inside, it is surprisingly large and opens onto a flowery terrace, veranda and views. The double room has powder blue walls and a patchwork quilt, the twin room a painted wood ceiling and antique beds. The mood is light and sunny; there are attractive colours and pale terracotta floor tiles. The large kitchen/living room is well equipped, and has pierced metalwork doors, a sofabed, armchairs and a big wooden table. Sophie's green fingers have surrounded the house with climbers and fragrant herbs – flowers peer in through every window, and it is a pleasure not knowing where the house ends and the garden begins. There is a splash pool close by and a small lake two minutes' away. Behind the house, on the edge of hills, is a eucalyptus plantation, olive groves, good walks (which Tuke will guide or provide maps for) and plenty of bird life. The coast is 12km away. *Note that a larger second house is also available in the village.*

**Rooms:** 1 with bath & wc, 2 rooms sharing shower & wc and 2 rooms with shared bath & wc.
**Price:** Double/Twin Esc 13,000; Apartment Esc 20,000.
**Breakfast:** Self-catering
**Meals:** Self-catering.
**Closed:** Never.

From Cercal, go south towards Odemira. Just after S. Luis go right at cemetary (sign Val Bejinha), after 2km turn right at small white cottage, up rough track, left at top.

**Map no: 5**

**Entry no: 129**

# Quinta do Barranco da Estrada

7665 – 880 Santa Clara a Velha  **Tel:** 283 933901
Alentejo                         **Fax:** 283 933901
                                 **E-mail:** paradiseinportugal@mail.telepac.pt
                                 **Web:** www.paradise-in-portugal.com

**Lulu & Frank McClintock**

Hugging the shore of one of the Alentejo's largest freshwater lakes, Barranco da
Estrada is ideal if you love wild beauty, and are looking for a real hideaway. The
whole area has a micro-climate which keeps the water warm enough for a long
swimming season and nurtures an amazing range of plant and animal life; visit in
spring and the wild flowers will have you in raptures. Lulu and Frank spent a
decade renovating the original, low house and then added a row of guest rooms.
They are light, cool and uncluttered and their terraces all look towards the lake.
Lounge, dining room and bar share one large room and happily embrace
Portuguese and English styles of décor. Beyond huge windows there is a vine-
festooned terrace where you spend most of your time when it's warm. Above the
lake a series of terraces has been planted with hibiscus, oleander, palm, jasmine,
plumbago and cactus. A sinuous path cuts down through all this to the jetty where
you can canoe, fish for crayfish, sail, water-ski or walk the shoreline, perhaps in the
company of one of the McClintock's six dogs. Frank will help with the naming of
all those birds and, if you're lucky, you may see mongoose or wild boar.

**Rooms:** 7 with bath & wc.
**Price:** Single Esc 13,000-17,500;
Double/Twin Esc 15,000-22,000; Family
room (for 4) Esc 32,000-48,000.
**Breakfast:** Esc 1,000 (cooked breakfast).
**Meals:** Lunch Esc 3,000;
Dinner Esc 4,000.
**Closed:** Mid-November-mid February.

From Lisbon A2 towards Algarve and after
175km right towards Odemira then left to
S. Martinho das Amoreiras; here towards Portimão. At T-junction left to
Monchique; after 8km left to Cortes Pereiras; after 8.5km right to the Quinta.

# Monte da Moita Nova

Cavaleiro
7630-055 Odemira
Algarve

**Tel:** 283 647357
**Fax:** 283 647167
**E-mail:** moitanova@mail.telepac.pt

**Ute Gerhardt**

If horse-riding and unspoilt beaches are your pleasure, stay a week with Ute and Walter at their Alentejo farm. This is an exceptionally beautiful and unspoilt part of Portugal's Atlantic coastline which has recently been designated a National Park; the ecosystem of the dunes nurtures a huge variety of plant and animal life. You can reach them, and hidden coves beyond, by walking just 300 yards across Cavaleiro's pastures. The original farmhouse has two apartments and a large guest lounge; the other two have been newly built and horseshoe around a central swathe of green. They are south-facing to catch the sun; each has its own terrace and woodburner and they have a fresh and uncluttered feel: you benefit from architect Walter's good use of space. Floors are of terracotta, sheets of good linen, beds of pine, and the kitchens have full self-catering kit. The buildings are softened thanks to a riot of climbers: a wonderful spot from which to watch the sun dipping into the Atlantic. It is nice to come across a place which is so friendly to children; there's a paddling pool, beach toys and games. Ride out from Cavaleiro on well-mannered thoroughbreds.

**Rooms:** 4 self-catering apartments.
**Price:** Double/Twin Esc 13,000;
Apartment Esc 20,000.
**Breakfast:** None available.
**Meals:** None available.
**Closed:** Never.

From Faro IC4 via Abufeira, Portimão and Lagos to Aljezur. Then N120 to S. Teotónio. Left here via Zambujeira to Cavaleiro. Here towards beach (not Cabo Sardão), and right after bridge to Moita Nova.

**Map no: 5**

Entry no: 131

# Inn Albergeria Bica-Boa

Estrada de Lisboa 266
8550 Monchique
Algarve

**Tel:** 282 912271
**Fax:** 282 912360
**E-mail:** enigma@mail.telepac.pt

**Susan Clare Cassidy**

Healing, visualisation, massage and meditation are among the offerings at Bica Boa, as is a good selection of vegetarian food, thanks to the interests of owner Susan, who has lived here for many years. Bica-Boa's name was inspired by the springs that well up on this wooded mountainside above Monchique; winding your way up from the western Algarve the exuberant vegetation of the place takes you by surprise. There are stunning walks galore and, if you venture up here, do stay at Bica-Boa. The hotel stands just to the side of the road but there is little traffic and the four guest rooms are tucked away to the rear of the building. They are fresh, light and simply decorated with wooden floors and ceilings – and all have views across the valley. There is a quiet little guest lounge with the same view; a corner chimney, *azulejo*-clad walls and a chess table give a homely feel. Bica Boa's restaurant is popular with locals and ex-pats up from the coast. Susan is adding more vegetarian dishes to the menu, and also a five-day detox programme. There are terraces for *al fresco* dining when the weather is right and a terraced garden with quiet corners for sitting out. Good for walks, too.

**Rooms:** 4 with bath & wc.
**Price:** Twin Esc 10,500-12,500.
**Breakfast:** Included.
**Meals:** Lunch/dinner Esc 3,000-5,000.
**Closed:** Never.

From Faro N125 west towards Lagos. Exit for Portimão/Monchique; to Monchique; follow signs to Lisboa through town. Bica-Boa is approx. 300m after leaving town on right; well signposted.

# Casa do Buraco

Estrada Perdida **Tel:** 123 456 7789
666 Boca do Inferno
Algarve

**Doug A. Hole**

Built by an ex-pat who couldn't stand the southern summer heat, this self-catering *casa* in unspoilt grounds has more to it than meets the eye. Go in through a plain-looking front door – its designer did not believe in fripperies – and into the small living/dining area: elegant white plastic table and chairs and classic small black & white TV may remind you of home. Twin porthole windows survey a desiccated landscape and admit minimum light. Swish through the traditional polythene bead curtain and be careful not to stumble: the bedroom is reached down a 250-foot, carved stone staircase. As you descend, candle in hand, so do the light and temperature, and at the bottom it is dank as you grope around for the bedroom door. Inside the pretty bunker-like room are two cream-painted tubular beds that hint at a medical history. Blow out your candle and you're either whisked into the arms of Morpheus or subject to terror, depending on how echoing drips affect you in total darkness. If you do need to go up to the bathroom, leave time for the climb, and, rising for breakfast, the relief at seeing blue sky again makes it all seem worthwhile, "like a resurrection" said our inspector (now retired).

**Rooms:** 1 with separate bath & wc.
**Price:** Toned calves, white hair;
2nd night free.
**Breakfast:** Never tasted better.
**Meals:** Stiff brandy.
**Closed:** Only to the timid.

Down the steps one at a time, and, further down, try not to lose your steps on slippery stones and wet moss.

# Corte Pero Jacques

Espinhaço de Cão
Bordeira
8670 Lagos
Algarve

**Tel:** 282 687893
**Fax:** 282 687893
**E-mail:** perojacques@teleweb.pt
**Web:** www.corteperojacques.pt

### Diogo Vasconcelos & António Malta

On a clear day you can see for miles and miles out across the surrounding
countryside and the protected western Vicentino coast. Corte Pero Jacques, an old
pink farmhouse which has been cleverly grafted onto a modern two-storey house,
has a truly spectacular setting, high on the Serra do Espinhaço de Cão ('dog's
spine') amid scrub and forests. The marriage of old and new is very effective. The
old house – two self-catering apartments – is decorated and furnished in
traditional, rustic Algarve style; the new part is white, sunny and harmonious. The
bedrooms have French windows onto balconies, and good beds and bathrooms.
Meals are served in the open-plan dining/living area; it has an open fireplace, rug-
strewn tiled floors, comfy sofas and French windows onto the terrace; this would
be a great place to relax after a meal of fresh fish cooked by António. Outside there
are hammocks, a barbecue, a children's play area and walks. Enthusiastic owners
Diogo and António both studied agriculture and have planted much of what
graces their 22 hectares of paradise, including stacks of flowers. The beaches are
10km away. A one-off, with wonderful location and atmosphere.

**Rooms:** 10, all with bath & wc; 2 apartments.
**Price:** Double/Twin Esc 13,000;
Apartment Esc 20,000.
**Breakfast:** Included.
**Meals:** Lunch on request; dinner
Esc 2,000-4000.
**Closed:** November.

From Lagos, after Bensafrim 15km, just before junction
sign to Sagres, opp. Taberna do Rosado, left into dirt
track, past watch tower, through eucalyptus plantation,
house signed, above on the right.

Entry no: 134                                                          Map no: 5

# Pensão Residência Dom Henrique

Sítio da Mareta                    **Tel:** 282 620000/3
8650-356 Sagres                    **Fax:** 282 620001/4
Algarve

**Ana Fernandes**

Sagres' claim to fame is that it was here, on this beautiful stretch of coast, that Henry the Navigator (Dom Henrique) set up his illustrious school many centuries ago, which led to Portugal's Discoveries and empire. Right in the centre of town, the Dom Henrique is a small, modern hotel where the sea-facing rooms have views and terraces that lift this hotel into the 'special' league. They are average-sized, irreproachably spic and span and have small bathrooms. They are fitted with pleasant wooden furniture and have good mattresses and bedding. It was wonderful to awake to a blushing dawn, to hear the crash of the waves and look out to the Atlantic sandwiched between headlands to the east and west. The Dom Henrique's lounge and dining room are light and simply furnished with wicker furniture and potted plants. The dining room gives onto a sea-fronting terrace where a bar serves sun-downers in the warmer months. The beach is just a couple of hundred yards away and so too are exhilarating walks – with superb views – along the cliff's edge. A place to breath sea air and feel inspired, as Dom Henrique was. This quiet little hotel is also great value out of season.

**Rooms:** 18 with bath & wc.
**Price:** Double/Twin Esc 5,000-15,500; Single Esc 4,000-13,000.
**Breakfast:** Included.
**Meals:** Lunch/Dinner available, from Esc 2,500.
**Closed:** Never.

As you enter Sagres, at the roundabout turn left. On arriving at a small square with café on the corner, turn right. Pensão at end on left.

**Map no: 5**                                    Entry no: 135

# Salsalito

Alagoas Burgau
Algarve

**Tel:** 282 697628 / 788272
**Fax:** 282 788272
**E-mail:** salsalito@clix.pt

### Ralph & Sally Everleigh

A dream home that Ralph and Sally have spent 12 years creating – it's high-quality 'Santa Fe', rustic in style, with chunky wood beams, half-tree trunk shelves and curious 'junk' collections. The guest book tells it like it is: "perfect", "wonderful" and "award yourself 20 stars". Sally will read your cards at the drop of a hat and Ralph is a master of all trades, including carpentry. He recycled timber to make wardrobes, tables and door lintels. The bar is well stocked, and only teetotallers will fail to enjoy its – and your hosts' – abundance. The lounge has a beamed ceiling and log fire for cooler nights. Outside, on hotter days, you can relax in the horseshoe-shaped cloister, festooned with bougainvillaea and enjoy the valley setting. Nearby, among attractive mixed trees, is the new pool. The bedrooms have a touch of British B&B, with kettles and teabags; the beds are comfy and the furniture handmade. You'll find plenty to do here, including sampling the Everleigh's wonderful Beach Bar and the bars and restaurants in Burgau – only 10 minutes away – which still retains its old fishing village character.

**Rooms:** 3 with bath & wc.
**Price:** Double/Twin Esc 13,000;
Apartment Esc 20,000.
**Breakfast:** Included.
**Meals:** None available.
**Closed:** November-March.

Turn left off the N125 for Almadena, then for Burgau. Look out for yellow balustrade, turn right immediately. If you reach the Pig's Head, you've gone too far.

# Monte Rosa

Lagoa da Rosa
8600-016 Barão de S. João
Algarve

**Tel:** 282 687002 688178
**Fax:** 282 687015
**E-mail:** monte.rosa@clix.pt
**Web:** www.home.zonnet.nl/monte-rosa

### Sandra Falkena

Ten-year-old Arianne loves to show other children the garden at Monte Rosa, the old farm complex run by her mother Sandra. In these 3.5 hectares of flourishing Algarve hinterland you can choose self-catering, B&B or camping under the almond, olive and fig trees. Near the house is a colourful garden with pathways, terraces and playground, and children will also love the cats, chickens, hamsters and rabbit. Sandra is Dutch and has converted Monte Rosa into apartments and rooms. The result is a well-organised, informal and friendly rural home where you have choices, such as private or shared bathrooms and common or private kitchens; all the rooms are simple and attractive, with lots of wood. Alternatively you can return to your tent or camper van (for campers there's a shared kitchen) or explore the gardens and salt-water pool. Monte Rosa is very informal. Sandra used to run a restaurant in Lagos, and four nights a week cooks Portuguese, international and vegetarian dinners; the food is delicious. The communal room, where you eat, has a bar, lovely pale terracotta sofas which match the floor and ochre sponged paintwork.

**Rooms:** 6 rooms with bath & wc and 2 sharing; apartment (available July-mid-September) sleeping 6-8 people.
**Price:** Single Esc 5,500-9,000; Double/Twin Esc 7,000-10,000; 3 people Esc 8-11,000; Apartment Esc 20,000 (min 2 nights).
**Breakfast:** Included.
**Meals:** Available four times a week Esc 2,500 (April-September).
**Closed:** Never.

From Lagos head for Aljezur; after 2km go through Portelas and at end of village go left to Barão de S. João. Monte Rosa is 4km on the left.

**Map no: 5**

# Quinta das Barradas

Odiáxere
8600 Lagos
Algarve

**Tel:** 282 770200
**Fax:** 282 770209

**Urs & Vera Wild**

Almost hidden in this agricultural landscape is this large farm with converted barns and outbuildings. It's beautiful, elegant and comfortable and is professionally-run by hotelier Urs and Vera, a friendly and gracious couple. Wherever you look there's a creative use of materials – carved stone, wood, old roof tiles, flagstones and cobbles. The main house is more like a Minho farmhouse, yet sits perfectly in this Algarve landscape. Bedrooms are traditional with tiled floors, scrolled wooden beds, wooden ceilings and excellent bathrooms. Each room has its own sitting area outside, so you can revel in privacy, too. The food is delicious and served on a heavy table in a room with a flagstone floor and candelabra; outside there's a roofed eating area. The Swiss chef offers international and Portuguese dishes, and most of the food is home-produced or local. Palm and fruit trees surround the farm and there's a spring which feeds pools via reed beds, plus a natural swimming pool. Horseriding is available at English stables nearby.

**Rooms:** 15: 2 with bath & wc, 13 with shower & wc.
**Price:** Double/Twin Esc 7,100-9,400; Single Esc 8,000-11,500; half board Esc 3,800.
**Breakfast:** Included.
**Meals:** Lunch from Esc 750; Dinner, 3-course, Esc 3,800.
**Closed:** Never.

From Odiáxere take the road out of the village to the barragem; at the windmill fork right and downhill, after 400m turn left (very small sign) and keep going to the end.

Entry no: 138

Map no: 5

168

# Quinta das Achadas

00351

Estrada da Barragem
Odiáxere
8600-251 Lagos
Algarve

**Tel:** 282 798425
**Fax:** 282 799162

**Beatrice & Willy Hagmann**

It took seven months of work from dawn to dusk for Willy and Beatrice to redecorate/convert the Quinta das Achadas. Hats off to this quiet-mannered Swiss couple for creating one of the best B&Bs of the Algarve. The approach is a delight: a winding drive through groves of olive, almond and orange trees which then give way to a wonderful subtropical garden where maguey and palm, geranium and bougainvillaea, pine and jasmine jostle for position; there is a new pool, too. The bedrooms, each with its own small terrace, look out across the gardens and are in the converted barn and stables; some have modern furniture, others antiques (our favourite is *Hibiscus*) and the innumerable South American bits and bobs are mementoes from Willy's work in those parts. In colder weather you breakfast in a cosy dining room (it doubles as a bar – just help yourself) but most of the year it's mild enough to sit out on the terrace; try the 'gourmet breakfast' and you'll be hooked. If you're in any of the the five apartments you can prepare your own food; the spacious *Bougain-Villa* (sic) with its beautiful bathroom and grand sitting room was our favourite, but all are special.

**Rooms:** 3 with bath & wc; 3 apartments.
**Price:** Double/Twin Esc 10,000-14,000 inc. breakfast; Apartment Esc 14,500-20,500 (min. 3 nights).
**Breakfast:** Included. Esc 1,200 if in Apartment.
**Meals:** None available.
**Closed:** November-mid March.

From Portimão, N125 towards Lagos. In village of Odiáxere, right at sign for Barragem. House signposted on right after 1.2km.

**Map no: 5**

Entry no: 139

# Quinta da Alfarrobeira

Estrada do Palmares
Odiáxere
8600 Lagos
Algarve

**Tel:** 282 798424
**Fax:** 282 799630
**E-mail:** bakker@mail.telepac.pt

### Theo Bakker & Inge Keizer

For the young family from Holland, now embellishing their dream home, it was love at first sight. Quinta da Alfarrobeira stands on a hill just inland from the Algarve coast and is surrounded by six hectares of old fruit groves. You might be fired by similar dreams as you sit beneath the enormous *alfarrobeira* (carob) and gaze out across the old olive and almond trees, or watch the three sons playing happily with their adopted pets on a sunny flower-filled patio. Choose between a room in the main house or one of two guest houses built in traditional Algarve style where terracotta, beam and bamboo are the essential ingredients. We loved their light, airy feel and the antique furnishings that have been collected piecemeal from all over Europe. There are biggish bathrooms, private terraces and views – and kitchens in the guest houses if you plan to cook for yourself. Add to this the lovely walks out from the quinta (just 1.5km down to the sea), exceptionally kind hosts and you begin to get the measure of this entirely special place.

**Rooms:** 1 with bath & wc; 2 guesthouses.
**Price:** Double Esc 13,000; 'Stable' Apartment Esc 9000-15,000; 'Farmhouse' Apartment Esc 90,000-180,000.
**Breakfast:** Self-catering
**Meals:** None – self-catering.
**Closed:** Never.

From Faro m'way (E1) then N125 to Portimão and on towards Lagos. In village of Odiáxere left at square towards Meia praia/Palmares. After 1.3km (cow sign on right) turn left; first house on right.

# Casa da Palmeirinha

Rua da Igreja, 1
Mexilhoeira Grande
8500 Portimão
Algarve

**Tel:** 282 969277
**Fax:** 282 969277
**E-mail:** josejudice@mail.telepac.pt

**José Manuel Gonçalves
Júdice Glória**

This graceful old house may remind you of Seville or Morocco because it is centred on its inner courtyard and garden, and is much bigger than it seems from the outside. José, a newspaper columnist who speaks excellent English, is an entirely genial host and was born in the house, which was his grandfather's. The bedrooms have varied views of the church and village; our two favourites have access to a terrace and roof garden and views of the Alvor bird sanctuary. The Spanish-influenced sitting room has walls decorated with dark green and white tiles, a terracotta floor and rustic wooden furniture. Then there's the huge interior tiled patio with its ornamental pool, swimming pool and lawn, shaded by arching palms – a wonderful place to relax (you can make tea and coffee in the the kitchen). You may well meet the owners' friendly old Algarve water dogs and a Labrador. This is an unusual opportunity to stay in a truly Portuguese townhouse; a delight inside and out; the village too is genuinely Portuguese-Algarve and has the famous Vila Lisa restaurant. There's a bird sanctuary nearby and good walks.

**Rooms:** 3 with bath and 3 with shower & wc.
**Price:** Double/Twin Esc 7,500-18,000.
**Breakfast:** Included – Continental.
**Meals:** Dinner, with notice.
**Closed:** December.

From Portimão or Lagos on the N125, go into Mexilhoeira Grande until you reach the church; Casa de Palmeirinha is on your left, turn left.

Map no: 5                    Entry no: 141

# Quinta das Flores

Apartado 93
Mexilhoeira Grande
8500 Portimão
Algarve

**Tel:** 282 968 649
**Fax:** 282 969 293
**E-mail:** ghampadams@hotmail.com

### Gaelle & David Hamp-Adams

There is art in very fabric of the colourful Quinta of Flowers, because Gaelle and David, who farmed in Africa, are also landscape gardener and painter. The sculpted gardens have beautiful lawns, palms, pergolas of bougainvillaea, shady spots, plus tennis court, curved-sided pool, barbecue and bar. Inside this elegant Algarve house there is something colonial thanks to Gaelle's vibrant paintings of zebras and the landscapes of Africa and the Alentejo. There is a galleried sitting room and large, green-painted dining room, both with open fires for cooler seasons, an 'honesty' bar, terracotta floors strewn with rugs, cream walls and large, comfy sofas and chairs. There are also large wicker armchairs overlooking the garden. The West Wing cottage has double and twin bedrooms which, along with the Studio, are self-catering only. The Pool Room is a double with shower, close to the swimming pool. Décors are fresh and sunny, the beds are large and the atmosphere homelike. Gaelle prepares everything from Thai and Indian curries and vegetarian food to typical Portuguese, and breakfasts can be full English or Continental.

**Rooms:** 1 with shower & wc; Studio, with shower & wc; 2-bed cottage with bath & wc.
**Price:** Room Esc 10,000; Studio Esc 12,000; Cottage for 4 Esc 17,000.
**Breakfast:** Included or self-catering.
**Meals:** Lunch on request; Dinner, Esc 6,500, inc. wine.
**Closed:** Never.

From Portimão, go to Lagos, past Penina, turn right into Figueira. Go past church and just before pink Café Célia, turn right.

# Casa Três Palmeiras

Apartado 84
8501-909 Portimão
Algarve

**Tel:** 282 401275
**Fax:** 282 401029

**Dolly Schlingensiepen**

What a setting! From Casa Três Palmeiras' perch right at the cliff's edge the view is a symphony of sea, sky, and rock – ever-changing according to the day's mood and ever beautiful. The house was built in the Sixties, but the 'Zen' design still feels modern. It has a distinctly exotic feel thanks to three enormous palm trees and the simple arches that soften the façade and give welcome shade to the guest rooms once the temperature creeps up. Rooms have everything you might expect for the price. There are marble floors, double sinks and big, fitted wardrobes, yet they remain uncluttered. Best of all, they lead straight out onto the terrace whence those heavenly views (and a sea water pool). It is a very comfortable house and the service is warm and friendly. There are always freshly cut flowers and a bowl of fruit awaiting guests and it is obvious that Brazilian Dolly is happy in her role of hostess and that entertaining comes naturally to her. A path leads from the house straight down to the beach; get up early and even in midsummer you may find you have it to yourself. Book well ahead in summer. *Reduced green fees and car hire rates available for Três Palmeiras guests.*

**Rooms:** 5 with bath & wc.
**Price:** Double Esc 24,706-31,890;
Single Esc 21,274-28,509.
**Breakfast:** Included.
**Meals:** Meals & snacks available.
**Closed:** December 1-January 31.

From Portimão take dual carriageway towards Praia da Rocha. Right at last roundabout towards Praia do Vau; at next roundabout double back and turn up track on right after 100m. Right along track at first villa.

**Map no: 5**

# Casa Domilu

Estrada de Benagil
Alfanzina
8400 Carvoeiro
Algarve

**Tel:** 282 350610
**Fax:** 282 358410
**E-mail:** casa.domilu@mail.telepac.pt
**Web:** www.casa-domilu.com

### Abilio D'Almeida

Finally a place to stay in Portugal that is less than 200 years old! Abilio designed and built this pinky-beige villa as a holiday home for the family. Then the children grew up and he decided to extend it and this small, special hotel was born. If you wince at anything that smacks of kitsch then this is not for you. But it you don't, and are looking for a comfortable and friendly place to stay on the Algarve, then do give it a go. The décor of lounge and dining room is very pick-and-mix; there are repro antiques, Art-Deco-ish chairs, dragon-tooth floors and modern prints. An enormous sweep of glass in both rooms looks out to the pool. The bedrooms are big, light, cheerful and marble-floored and have all the swish extras: book the honeymoon suite and you get a sunken whirlpool bath surrounded by potted palms and Doric columns! Breakfast is a buffet: big and designed to please a northern European palate, while dinner is resolutely Portuguese. Try the *cataplana*, one of the Algarve's delicious seafood dishes. There is tennis, a sauna and mountain bikes. Guests, many of whom are German, return year after year.

**Rooms:** 24 with bath & wc; 6 suites.
**Price:** Double Esc 10,000-18,000;
Twin Esc 14,000-24,000;
Suite Esc 22,000-50,000.
**Breakfast:** Included.
**Meals:** Lunch Esc 2,000-3,500; Dinner
Esc 3,000-5,000.
**Closed:** Never.

From N125 exit for Carvoeiro and 200m
after Intermarché supermarket left at signs
for Casa Domilu.

# Quinta da Figueirinha

8300-028 Silves
Algarve

**Tel:** 282 440 700
**Fax:** 282 440 709
**E-mail:** qdf@qdf.pt
**Web:** www.qdf.pt

### Dr. Gerhard & Uta Ingeborg Zabel

What can be better than fresh organic food, open countryside and the Algarve climate? You approach through a lush, fruit-growing valley, past orange groves and loquat trees and then almond and carob trees as you rise to the Quinta. Here, surrounded by views of fields and orchards, is an organic farm with purpose-built 'cottages' and apartments for guests. Standing on a hill, above terraces of mature planting, bougainvillaea and geraniums, you can enjoy the best of nature. There are large irrigation tanks nearby for a quick plunge and there's a shop where you can buy fresh organic fruit and vegetables, carob bread, dried fruits, liqueurs and marzipan. Gerhard and Ute are pleased to explain the work of their farm and they and their four children, speak excellent English. There is a library in the training and seminar room and courses and guided tours are available on request. The décor here is plain and simple, nothing fussy; kitchens are well equipped. Perfect for people who want to eat as nature intended.

**Rooms:** 11 apartments (7 for 2; 4 for 4 people); guest house for 6.
**Price:** For 2 Esc 6,460-10,765; For 4 Esc 10,765-16,195; guest house Esc 12,915-19,375.
**Breakfast:** Esc 800.
**Meals:** None available.
**Closed:** Never

From Silves, cross the bridge and take first left. (From Faro, turn right just before the bridge, when you have Silves in view.) Follow signs to Fragura and then the winding road for Quinta da Figueirinha.

**Map no: 5**

# The Garden Cottages

8100 Loulé
Algarve

*Booked*

**Tel:** 0208 366 8944 (UK agent)

In a lush valley in the Algarve just a couple of miles back from the coast; long hours of sunshine and rich soil allow nearly everything to grow in profusion. The English owner found this old wine farm in ruins in the early '70s and has put in years of patient restoration and planting, and the results are delightful. This is a place of peace and privacy; behind the whitewashed outer wall the cottages stand apart from one another facing the gardens and – tucked away beyond – an enormous round swimming pool. Each cottage has a sun and a shade terrace, a prettily tiled kitchen, a sitting room and double bedroom – perfect for two. (The cottages are self-catering, but breakfast is also available.) Dried flowers, eucalyptus beams and terracotta give a 'country' feel, while mementoes from Africa and Turkey add an exotic note. There are magazines and a carefully compiled file with details of restaurants, shops and visits; you'll feel instantly at home. What we remember most are the gardens: olive, pomegranate, almonds and lemon and, beneath them, a profusion of flowers of every hue. The benign climate means that visiting out of season is just as special.

**Rooms:** 6 cottages with shower & wc and living room/kitchen.
**Price:** £200-£500, per week for two people (depending on cottage and season). Details on request.
**Breakfast:** Self-catering, or Continental can be arranged.
**Meals:** None – self-catering.
**Closed:** Never.

Information will be sent by UK agent (see above).

# Casa Belaventura

Campina de Boliqueime          **Tel:** 289 360633
8100-073 Loulé                 **Fax:** 289 366053
Algarve                        **E-mail:** belaventura@mail.telepac.pt

**Carlos Dias**

Belaventura lies deep in the Algarve hinterland; in such a pastoral setting you can soon forget that the highway and the busy coastal towns of Vilamoura and Albufeira are close by. Carlos converted this old farmhouse with B&B and self-catering in mind; as well as a beautifully proportioned sitting room there is a large dining room and fully equipped kitchen. The house is light and airy by the open arches that link the spaces; a more traditional Algarve style is present in the terracotta floor, wafer brickwork and marvellously weathered roof tiles. Carlos has given the building extra volume and more modern lines by extending the roof outwards thus creating a shady outside sitting area. By the pool in the garden there's a hammock in the shade of an olive tree and beyond it, through the almond groves, you catch glimpses of the glittering sea. The bedrooms have contemporary paintings (some by Carlos' wife), durries, more traditional beam and bamboo roofs, perhaps a rattan chair or view across the garden. One is more of a suite with its own sitting room and inglenook. Carlos has a boat and can take you for a day's sailing along the Algarve coast.

**Rooms:** 5 with bath or shower & wc.
**Price:** Single Esc 9,000-15,000; Double Esc 10,500-17,000.
*Public holidays extra 20%.*
**Breakfast:** Included.
**Meals:** None available.
**Closed:** November-February.

From Faro towards Spain on IP1 motorway. Exit for Boliqueime and after just 250m turn right and Belaventura signposted on right after approx 750m.

**Map no: 5**                                    Entry no: 147

# Quinta da Calma

Apt. 3053
8135-901 Almancil
Algarve

**Tel:** 289 393 741
**Fax:** 289 393 346
**E-mail:** syltal@mail.telepac.pt

**Sylta Kalmbach**

Umbrella pines, an organic garden and 11 acres of sandy Algarve landscape surround this centre for yoga, holistic healing and learning. The Quinta, although close to the main road and airport, is surprisingly quiet, and was established a decade ago by Sylta, a calm and graceful woman who teaches yoga and meditation. She began it as a place for healthy holidays, now there's a wide range of alternative/complementary activities; it also welcomes people who want simply to relax. Guests can stay in the dormitory, where there is little privacy, but we prefer the four Rondettes, rustic-style wooden cabins each with a small living room and one bedroom, a single bed in each room, and a bathroom. These are simply furnished, as is the separate cottage with two single bedrooms and a veranda overlooking the valley. A new dormitory block has double and single rooms, but thin walls do not give much insulation. Elsewhere you can visit the large meeting house, with windows all round, and the vegetarian restaurant, both spaces octagonal and built in wood; there is also a covered terrace for eating outside. The mood is of peace and purpose.

**Rooms:** 4 cabins, 1 cottage and 2 dormitories with shared bathrooms.
**Price:** Double/Twin Esc 13,000; Apartment Esc 20,000.
**Breakfast:** Self-catering, unless on course.
**Meals:** Available during courses.
**Closed:** Christmas.

The Quinta is off the EN125 on the Faro side of Almancil. A small track opposite the cemetary of S. Lourenço leads to the Quinta. The track is between a car sales site and a yard selling logs; watch the road markings and don't cross the solid white line.

# Monte do Casal

Estoi
8000-661 Faro
Algarve

**Tel:** 289 991503/990140
**Fax:** 289 991341

### Bill Hawkins

After more than a dozen years at the helm, Bill Hawkins has firmly established Monte do Casal's credentials as one of the Algarve's special small hotels. This former farmhouse is hidden away in the gentle hills of the Algarve hinterland, a low, white building surrounded by exuberant stands of bougainvillaea, mature palms, olives and almonds. Inside, the eucalyptus and cane roofing and the terracotta floor tiles create an unmistakably Mediterranean atmosphere. Food is a cornerstone of the hotel's fame; Bill trained in the kitchens of Claridges and the Savoy and his house specialities and well-stocked wine cellar make a formidable partnership. However, if you do fancy a change, ask for his 'cryptic-map-guide to the Algarve'; it will lead you towards treasures you would otherwise miss, and picnic hampers can be provided to accompany your forays. The guest bedrooms have fine old brass cornered 'military' furniture and all have private terraces (where you can breakfast) overlooking the pool and gardens. But do book early, especially if planning a visit in season. *Children over 16 welcome.*

**Rooms:** 8 with bath & wc; 5 suites.
**Price:** Twin Esc 21-36,500; 'Deluxe' Esc 23,000-42,500; Suite Esc 28,000-50,000.
**Breakfast:** Included.
**Meals:** Lunch/Dinner Esc 3,700-5,000.
**Closed:** December & January.

From Faro take N2 north towards São Bras. Exit for Estoi. Here at square take road towards Moncarapacho; hotel is approx 2.5km along this road signposted to left.

**Map no: 6**

# Quinta da Belgica

Sítio da Fornalha
8700 Moncarapacho
Algarve

**Tel:** 289 791193
**Fax:** 289 791192
**E-mail:** jef.cloots@mail.telepac.pt
**Web:** www.quinta-da-belgica.com

### Mieke Everaert & Jef Cloots

Almost hidden by luxuriant trees and climbers, this two-storey, purpose-built holiday complex is perfect for families with young children. The atmosphere created by Mieke and Jef is casual and relaxed and since they bought the Quinta two years ago have been steadily brightening up the rooms. Bedrooms are basic rather than luxurious, with tiled floors, stripey curtains and aluminium doors which double as windows but you probably won't spend much time in your room because life here revolves around the pool and gardens. There is almost a hectare of ground with masses of flowers and plenty of shady spots beneath the palm, orange, almond and pepper trees. There are tables shaded by a bamboo roof and near the pool is a combined bar, lounge and dining room with a big squashy sofa and armchairs and a woodburning stove for cooler evenings. Mieke cooks both Portuguese and Northern European dishes. There is ping-pong and table football, and children will love playing with a collection of dressing-up clothes. The beaches are only 5km away and transport is easily arranged.

**Rooms:** 14 doubles (6 for families, with bunks) and 3 twins, with shower & wc.
**Price:** Double Esc 10,000 (Esc 20,000 inc. dinner); children under 6 free.
**Breakfast:** Included.
**Meals:** Dinner Esc 5,000 including drinks and aperitif. Snacks also available.
**Closed:** Never.

From Moncarapacho, take road to Olhão. After sharp bend, you'll see the entrance marked with flags.

Entry no: 150

Map no: 6

# Hortanova

Machados                              **Tel:** 289 841020
Apt. 149
8150 São Bras de Alportel
Algarve

### Sue & Reg Hocking

Lying in a drowsy valley of olive groves, Hortanova is a homely, single-storey smallholding with white walls and blue-bordered windows. Here you can smell the earth and let life slow down, and as it is self-catering you can choose what time you rise to enjoy your breakfast in the sun. The sitting room has a lived-in feeling, as Reg and Sue, a generous, friendly couple, use it themselves in the winter if the cottage isn't rented. The tile floor is strewn with rugs and there is a pine table and dresser, comfy armchairs and a woodburner, so it will be cosy on winter evenings. You sleep in twin brass beds in a room of generous size, and there's a small shower room. The kitchenette, where you'll find a welcoming hamper, opens onto a walled, private patio, a sun trap with tables, chairs and umbrella. The guest area is marked by a rustic fence, but its very much part of Reg and Sue's farmhouse. This friendly, generous couple have a family of cats and dogs who are equally welcoming. If you need anything, Reg and Sue are on hand, but you can also be private. If you have young children, baby-sitting is available. The setting is lovely and in Algarve terms they're only 20 minutes from everywhere.

**Rooms:** 1-bedroom cottage.
**Price:** Double/Twin Esc 13,000;
Apartment Esc 20,000.
**Breakfast:** Self-catering.
**Meals:** Self-catering.
**Closed:** Never

From Faro follow signs to São Bras de Alportel. At Machados turn right towards Barracha. When you reach a fork, turn right (Estoi, Faro, Murta), then immediately right again, past football pitch; 2nd house on the left.

# Quinta Fonte do Bispo

Estrada National 270          **Tel:** 281 971484
Fonte do Bispo              **Fax:** 281 971484
8800-161 Tavira            **E-mail:** info@qtfontebispo.com
Algarve                    **Web:** www.qtfontebispo.com

### Jaime da Silva Brito Neto

The benign climate, exceptional vegetation, closeness to the sea and interesting folk architecture mean that the gentle hills of the Algarve hinterland remain a good choice for a holiday. This old farmstead will draw you deep into an affection for the region. It is a long, low, white building with pretty chimney stacks and broad bands of blue around doors and windows – typical of the area. Parts of the farm are 200 years old but it has been completely renovated. The six apartments in the converted outbuildings of the farm, fronting a cobbled central patio, were designed with families in mind: open-plan sitting rooms have beds which double up as sofas and there is a small kitchenette (useful for heating a bottle or making a cup of tea). The style is local and 'country'; the (herringbone) terracotta floor, beamed and bamboo roof and simple yet adequate shower rooms. There is a large communal sitting room in similar style but most of the year you will be out by the pool; find a shady spot beneath the orange, almond or olive trees. You can also enjoy a sauna, table-tennis, pool and a mini-gym. We could see why painting courses are held here.

**Rooms:** 6 apartments each sleeping up to 5 people.
**Price:** Double/Twin Esc 13,000; Apartment Esc 20,000.
**Breakfast:** Included.
**Meals:** On request approx. Esc 3,500.
**Closed:** Never

From Faro towards Spain on IP1. Pass Loulé then exit for Olhão/Santa Catarina. Arriving in Santa Catarina right towards Tavira. Quinta signposted on left after approx. 1km.

# Monte Mariposa

Apartado 57
8800 Tavira
Algarve

**Tel:** 281 971615
**Fax:** 281 971420
**E-mail:** montemariposa@mail.telepac.pt
**Web:** www.montemariposa.pt

**Dieter Gabriel Loomans**

This place is ideal for those with artistic and spiritual interests, for individuals, who will meet like-minded souls, and for groups and families. Meditation, shamanism, reiki, healing and other personal courses are organised at Monte Mariposa, a centre for arts and spiritual development. It is a new complex with a light and peaceful mood. Founders Gabriel Loomans and Angelina Atayde organise performances, courses and workshops covering art, dance, movement, holistic healing, theatre, music and environmental awareness, so if you want, and book in advance, you can have a very different kind of holiday. There is a fascinating library, a solar-heated pool, winter sauna and walks. The atmosphere is uplifting, with light colours, plenty of wood and vivid paintings, and lots of space. There is a large gathering room with wide views, and another room with a stage for theatre and music. The bedrooms are simply decorated, and range from a dormitory to apartments in the main house; there is also a separate house nearby. Outside there are sun terraces, hammocks to relax in, and the Algarve climate rarely disappoints.

**Rooms:** 6 2-bed apartments & 1-bed house with studio.
**Price:** Esc 8,000-10,000.
**Breakfast:** Yes, for more than 4 people, Esc 500.
**Meals:** Vegetarian lunch and dinner at weekends, Esc 1,500.
**Closed:** Never.

From São Bras de Alportel towards Tavira, through Santa Catarina 2km to Fonte de Bispo. Look out for 'Turismo Rural' painted on wall, go to next left, where there is triangular sign for Monte Mariposa. Go to top of hill.

**Map no: 6**                    Entry no: 153

# Quinta da Lua

Bernardinheiro 1622-X
S. Estevão
8800-513 Tavira
Algarve

**Tel:** 281 961070
**Fax:** 281 961070
**E-mail:** quintalua@oninet.pt

### Miguel Martins & Vimal Willems

Miguel and Vimal have stacks of enthusiasm for looking after people, and staying at their 'farm of the moon' is delightful on many levels. The food is especially good; Vimal is a professional chef who cooks 'global kitchen' and Mediterranean, (including imaginative vegetarian) dishes. Breakfast is different every day, and guests are asked their preferences; we noticed one enjoying beautifully arranged fruit one morning whilst sitting out under the green umbrella. The house is a two-storey addition to an old Algarve farmhouse, surrounded by orange trees and vineyards, carob, oleander, bougainvillaea and palms; there is a lovely pool with shaded verandas to the the side. Inside, you find a successful blend of modern and traditional décor, of rough terracotta floor tiles and beamed ceilings. The bedrooms and beds are big, colour-co-ordinated and well insulated against noise. The Lua logo is in two colours in bathrooms, so you won't use your room-mate's towel by mistake. "It was," said our inspector, "a delightful surprise to find such a special place so close to the island beaches. I loved it." And so, we think, will you.

**Rooms:** 8 with bath/shower & wc.
**Price:** Double/Twin Esc 9,000-14,000.
**Breakfast:** Included.
**Meals:** Lunch, dinner prepared 2/3 times a week, Esc 2,500.
**Closed:** Never.

From Faro, on N125 to Tavira. At main crossroads, left to S. Estevão. Take first left and next right, and look for arch over the Quinta gateway.

# Quinta do Caracol

Bairro de San Pedro
8800 Tavira
Algarve

**Tel:** 281 322475
**Fax:** 281 323175

**Susel and João Viegas**

"Around every corner a picture postcard", said an English couple staying here, and this was no understatement. Caracol means 'snail', and you see the spirals as you pass the blue and white entrance arch. Next you see a beautiful 17th-century farm in blue and white, its old outbuildings now high-quality accommodation. This blends traditional, aesthetic and practical concerns, and there is a pleasing use of colour and *azulejos* (rough terracotta tiles), chunky pillars and wooden beams. There is colourful planting in the garden, and clay pots and curved walls lend more interest. There is an attractive *tanque* for swimming, a round pond and a *nora* (well). Bedrooms are named after flowers and are cosy and traditional, with comfortable beds, fine bedcovers and furniture; each has a kitchenette and outdoor area for eating. There are many outside sitting areas as well as a canvas-covered dining room where you can sample local and vegetarian food. The name perhaps reflects the pace of life here in days gone by; now the house is on the edge of Tavira, which means a little traffic noise in the garden, but a short walk into town.

**Rooms:** 7 with bath & wc.
**Price:** Available on request.
**Breakfast:** Included
**Meals:** Available by arrangement.
**Closed:** Never

From Faro, turn right for Tavira and right again just before level crossing, and you see the white and blue arch and azulejo sign of Quinta do Caracol.

**Map no: 6**

Entry no: 155

# Convento do Santo António

Atalaia, Nº 56                    **Tel:** 281 321573
8800 Tavira                       **Fax:** 281 325632
Algarve

**Isabel Maria Castanho Paes**

Monks of the Capuchin order built the convent of Santo António and its
diminutive cloister; they chose a windswept place of rare beauty. Isabel is almost
apologetic that "the home has only been in the family for five generations". A
portrait of great-grandmother officiates over one of the vaulted corridors that runs
the length of the cloister (Santo Antonio looks benignly on from his chapel at the
end of the other) and it was grandfather, much travelled, who planted the exotic
garden. Here are rooms to remember; varying in size (and price) they have great
charm; here a vaulted ceiling, there a fine dresser; here a seaward view, there a
hand-knotted rug. It is a Lusitanian feast of hand-crafted terracotta and ceramic
tiles, of rich *alcobaça* fabrics and carefully chosen (often naïve) paintings. We loved
the Chapel room (one of two 'specials') with its high ceilings and bathroom sitting
snugly inside what once was a chimney breast. Lounge and bar are just as special
and it would be heavenly to breakfast in summer with Gregorian chant to
accompany your feast. And such a peaceful place. *Minimum stay Oct-Mar 2 nights;*
*April-June 3 nights; June-Aug 4 nights; Sep-Oct 3 nights.*

**Rooms:** 6 with bath & wc; 1 suite.
**Price:** Double/Twin Esc 17,000-21,000; 'Special'
Double/Twin Esc 19,000-24,000; Suite Esc 28,000-
32,500
**Breakfast:** Included – buffet.
**Meals:** Dinner on request, Esc 4,000.
**Closed:** January.

From Faro, N125 then m'way IP1 towards Espanha.
Exit 7 to Tavira. Here, under archway to r'bout and
straight on towards 'Centro Saude'. On, over T-
junction; once past church right towards 'Cento Saude'.
Bear right past army barracks, then first left; after 200m
fork right to Convento. Or ask a local!

Entry no: 156                                   **Map no: 6**

# Casa Nossa Senhora do Carmo

Rua do Pópulo de Cima, Nº 220      **Tel:** 296 642048
Livramento                          **Fax:** 296 642038
9500 Ponta Delgada                  **E-mail:** carmo@virtualazores.com
São Miguel

**Maria do Carmo Homem de F. da Conceição Santos**

The Azores are some of the world's most beautiful islands, and this house is one of
their gems, a long, white 17th-century manor full of character, run by a warm and
caring hostess. Maria do Carmo, who was born in the house, restored it from a
near-ruin in the early 1980s, and has done it beautifully, with real attention to
detail. Surrounded by a simple yet luxuriant garden and an orchard of citrus and
exotic fruit trees, the house is full of character, of surprises even, and good, natural
materials have been used throughout. The large bedrooms are all different; the
beds have ornate headboards and the windows lovely views over the gardens. The
general style is rustic and traditional and the long lounge, an enormous room, has
a wonderful beamed ceiling, a wide fireplace, bar and lots of seating. There's a
large dining room with wooden ceiling, old oil paintings and display cabinets, and
a beamed-ceiling kitchen and breakfast room, where the heavy wood table and
benches are supported on blocks of granite. Maria do Carmo is quite a collector of
antiques, and wherever you look there are fascinating things, many of them family
heirlooms. Outside, there are beautiful beaches close by.

**Rooms:** 6 with bath & wc.
**Price:** Double/Twin Esc 17,000;
Single Esc 15,000.
**Breakfast:** Included.
**Meals:** Dinner, with notice, from
Esc 4,200.
**Closed:** December.

From Ponte Delgada airport head for
Livramento, 5km away, and look for signs
to the house.

**Map no: 5**                              Entry no: 157

# Casa das Calhetas

Rua da Boa Viagem
Calhetas
9600-016 Ribeira Grande
São Miguel

**Tel:** 296 498120
**Fax:** 296 498199
**E-mail:** e.regogonzalez@mail.telepac.pt
**Web:** www.virtualazores.com/turismo/casacalhetas

### Carlos Diez Gonzalez

On the island of São Miguel, this house has been in the same family since it was built in 1723. Margarida's family were farmers and wine-producers, and today she and her Spanish husband Carlos run their old granite house partly as a guest house. You enter through an impressive portico into the front courtyard, around which the house is built on three sides. The front of the house looks out over the Atlantic and from the rooms and balcony you see unlimited ocean and, to the side, the rocky outline of the Serra da Lagoa do Fogo (Lake of Fire). At the back, facing south-west, the guest rooms survey the beautiful garden of mature trees and plants, many of them specimens brought back long ago from other lands, and the island's old convent and cloister. The house is simple and colonial in style, typically Azorean, and the furniture and beds, while old, are solid and not overly ornate. It is very much a family home, with a feeling of calm. The sea is close by and the climate here is generally very mild. There are wonderful walks to be walked, a fishing port and some good seafood restaurants 2km away. Come and explore the islands from here.

**Rooms:** 3 with bath & wc.
**Price:** Double/Twin Esc 12,000-16,000; Single Esc 14,000.
**Breakfast:** Included.
**Meals:** None available.
**Closed:** Never.

# Vocabulary for dining out

## Basics

| | | | |
|---|---|---|---|
| *Acepipes/entrados* | Hors d'oeuvres | *Arroz* | Rice |
| *Azeitonas* | Olives | *Manteiga* | Butter |
| *Ovos* | Eggs | *Pão* | Bread |
| *Pimenta* | Pepper | *Sal* | Salt |
| *Salada* | Salad | *Queijo* | Cheese |

## In restaurants

| | | | |
|---|---|---|---|
| *Almoço* | Lunch | *Colher* | Spoon |
| *Conta* | The bill | *Copo* | Glass |
| *Ementa* | Menu | *Faca* | Knife |
| *Garfo* | Fork | *Garrafa* | Bottle |
| *Jantar* | Dinner | *Pequeno almoço* | Breakfast |

## Meat, Poultry and Game

| | | | |
|---|---|---|---|
| *Borrega* | Lamb | *Cabrito* | Kid |
| *Carne de porco* | Pork | *Carneiro* | Mutton |
| *Coelha* | Rabbit | *Dobrada* | Tripe |
| *Galinha* | Chicken | *Morcelo* | Blood pudding |
| *Pato* | Duck | *Perú* | Turkey |
| *Salsicha* | Sausage | *Vitela* | Veal |

## Fish and Shellfish

| | | | |
|---|---|---|---|
| *Ameijos* | Clams | *Anchovas* | Anchovies |
| *Atum* | Tuna | *Camarões* | Shrimp |
| *Caranguejo* | Crab | *Gambas* | Prawns |
| *Lagosta* | Lobster | *Lulas* | Squid |
| *Mezilhões* | Mussels | *Ostras* | Oysters |
| *Polvo* | Octopus | *Salmão* | Salmon |
| *Sardinhas* | Sardines | *Truta* | Trout |

## Vegetables

| | | | |
|---|---|---|---|
| *Alcachofra* | Artichoke | *Alface* | Lettuce |
| *Alho* | Garlic | *Batatas* | Potatoes |
| *Cebola* | Onion | *Cenoura* | Carrot |
| *Cogumelos* | Mushrooms | *Ervilhas* | Peas |
| *Esparagos* | Asparagus | *Espinafre* | Spinach |
| *Favas* | Broad beans | *Pepino* | Cucumber |

## Specialities

*Açorda (de marisco)* - bread-based stew (cooked with spices and shellfish)
*Arroz de marisco* - seafood paella
*Bife à Portuguesa* - Beef steak, topped with mustard sauce and a fried egg
*Cataplana* - Lamb or kid casserole
*Espedeta mista* - Mixed meat kebab
*Frango na churrasca* - Barbecued chicken
*Leitão assado* - Roast suckling pig

# Useful vocabulary

### Before Arriving (therefore over the telephone).

| | |
|---|---|
| Do you have a room for the night? | *Tem um quarto para esta noite?* |
| How much does it cost? | *Quanto custa?* |
| We'll be arriving at about 7pm. | *Nós chegaremos por volta das sete da tarde.* |
| We're lost! | *Estamos perdidos!* |
| We'll be arriving late. | *Vamos chegar tarde.* |
| I'm in the phone box at... | *Estou na cabine telefónica em...* |
| I'm in the 'Oporto' bar in... | *Estou no bar 'Oporto' em...* |
| Do you have any animals? | *Você tem algum animal?* |
| I'm allergic to cats. | *Sou alérgico a gatos.* |
| We would like to have dinner. | *Queríamos jantar.* |

### On arrival.

| | |
|---|---|
| Hello! I'm Mr/Mrs X. | *Olá! eu sou o Senhor/Senhora X.* |
| We found your name in this book. | *Encontramos o seu nome neste livro.* |
| Where can we leave the car? | *Onde podemos deixar o carro?* |
| Could you help us with our bags? | *Podia ajudar-nos com as nossas malas?* |
| Could I leave this picnic food in your fridge? | *Podia deixar estas garrafas para picnic no seu frigorífico?* |
| Could I heat up the baby's bottle? | *Podia aquecer o biberon?* |
| How much will you charge for that? | *Quanto é que você cobrará por isto?* |

### Things that you need/that go wrong.

| | |
|---|---|
| Do you have an extra pillow/blanket? | *Você tem uma outra almofada/um outro cobertor?* |
| A light bulb needs replacing. | *É preciso mudar uma lampada.* |
| The heating isn't on. | *O aquecedor não está ligado.* |
| We've a problem with the plumbing. | *Temos um problema com a canalização.* |
| How does the air conditioning work? | *Como funciona o ar condicionado?* |
| The room smells! | *O quarto cheira mal!* |
| Do you have a quieter room? | *Tem um quarto menos barulhento?* |
| Where can I hang these wet clothes? | *Onde posso secar estas roupas?* |
| Could we have some soap? | *Queríamos sabonete por favor?* |
| Could you turn the volume down? | *Pode baixar o volume?* |
| Please could you give us some hot water to make tea - we have our own tea bags! | *Podia nos dar água quente para o nosso chá - temos as nossas próprias saquetas de chá.* |

### How the house/hotel works

| | |
|---|---|
| When do you begin serving breakfast? | *A que horas começa a servir o pequeno almoço?* |
| We'd like to order some drinks. | *Queríamos tomar algumas bebidas, por favor.* |
| Can the children play in the garden? | *As crianças podem brincar no jardim?* |
| Is there any danger? | *É perigoso?* |
| Can we leave the children with you? | *Podemos deixar as crianças convosco?* |

# Useful vocabulary

## Local Information

| | |
|---|---|
| Where can we buy petrol? | *Onde fica a próxima estação de serviço?* |
| How far is the nearest shop? | *Fica muito longe a próxima loja?* |
| We need a doctor. | *Precisamos dum médico.* |
| Where is the chemist's? | *Onde há uma farmácia?* |
| Where is the police station? | *Onde fica o posto de policia?* |
| Where's a good place to eat? | *Onde há um sítio onde se coma bem?* |
| Where can we find a cash-dispenser? | *Onde há uma caixa automática?* |
| Do you know of any local festivities? | *Sabe de algumas festividades locais?* |

## On leaving.

| | |
|---|---|
| What time must we leave the room? | *A que horas temos de libertar/deixar o quarto?* |
| We'd like to pay the bill. | *Queriamos pagar a conta.* |
| How much do I owe you? | *Quanto devo?* |
| We hope to be back. | *Esperamos regressar.* |
| We've had a very pleasant stay. | *Tivemos uma estadia muito agradável.* |
| This is a beautiful spot. | *Este é um lugar muito bonito.* |
| Thank you so much. | *Muito obrigado/a.* |

## Eating out (or in).

| | |
|---|---|
| Where's there a good bar? | *Onde há um bom bar?* |
| Could we eat outside, please? | *Podemos comer lá fora?* |
| What's today's set menu? | *Qual é o menu para hoje?* |
| What do you recommend? | *O que nos recomenda?* |
| What vegetarian dishes do you have? | *Que pratos vegetarianos tem?* |
| Do you have a wine list? | *Tem uma lista de vinhos?* |
| This food is cold! | *Esta comida está fria.* |
| Do you have some salt please? | *Tem sal por favor?* |
| What tapas do you have? | *Que aperitivos tem?* |
| A plate of this one. | *Uma dosa deste.* |
| Please keep the change. | *Guarde o troco.* |
| Where are the toilets? | *Onde ficam as casas de banho?* |
| The toilet is locked. | *As casas de banho estão fechadas.* |
| It was a delicious meal. | *Foi uma óptima refeição.* |
| I'd like a white coffee | *Queria um café com leite* |
| black coffee | *café simples* |
| weaker coffee | *café fraco* |
| coffee with just a little milk | *café com um pouco de leite* |
| tea** | *chá* |
| camomile tea | *chá de camomila* |

**remember, the safest way to order tea with milk is to ask for *um chá e um pouco de leite, mas aparte*. It's tempting to ask for *chá com leite* - but you may well end up with a glass of hot milk with a teabag plonked on the top! Milk is nearly always UHT so if you really need your tea we recommend drinking it with a slice of lemon *chá com limão*. Or take your own along and just ask for *jarro com água quente* in the bar. Your request will rarely be refused.

# Quick reference indices

## WHEELCHAIR

These owners have told us that they have facilities for people in wheelchairs. It is essential that you confirm what is available before arrival.

### Northern Portugal
Minho
3 • 4 • 5 • 10 • 15 • 18 • 19 • 20
Tràs-os-montes
26 • 28 •
Douro
32 • 36 • 41

### Central Portugal
Beira
45 • 49 • 50 • 52 • 55 • 58 • 59 • 61 • 66
Estremadura
69 • 73 • 74 • 77 • 81
Ribatejo
90 • 92 • 95 • 96 • 97 • 100

### Southern Portugal
Alentejo
103 • 107 • 109 • 110 • 111 • 115 • 118 • 120
Algarve
131 • 132 • 133 • 134 • 144 • 149 • 153

## ACCESS

These houses have bedrooms or bathrooms that are accessible for people of limited mobility. Please confirm details and special needs.

### Northern Portugal
Minho
1 • 12 • 13 • 22
Tràs-os-montes
25 • 29 •
Douro
39 • 43 • 44

### Central Portugal
Ribatejo
91 • 93 • 102

### Southern Portugal
Alentejo
121 • 130 •
Algarve
137 • 147 • 152

## SWIMMING POOL

These places have a pool on the premises.

### Northern Portugal
Minho
1 • 3 • 4 • 5 • 7 • 8 • 9 • 11 • 12 • 13 • 15 • 16 • 17 • 20 • 21 • 22 • 23
Tràs-os-montes
24 • 25 • 27 • 28 • 29 • 30 • 31
Douro
32 • 33 • 34 • 36 • 37 • 38 • 39 • 40 • 41

### Central Portugal
Beira
46 • 47 • 48 • 49 • 51 • 52 • 53 • 54 • 55 • 56 • 58 • 59 • 63 • 65 • 66
Estremadura
67 • 69 • 71 • 72 • 73 • 74 • 77 • 78 • 81 • 88
Ribatejo
90 • 91 • 92 • 93 • 94 • 95 • 96 • 99 • 100 • 101 • 102

### Southern Portugal
Alentejo
103 • 106 • 108 • 109 • 110 • 113 • 115 • 116 • 117 • 118 120 • 121 • 125 • 130
Algarve
132 • 134 • 136 • 137 • 138 • 139 • 140 • 141 • 142 • 143 • 144 • 145 • 146 • 147 • 148

# Quick reference indices

149 • 150 • 152 • 153 • 154
• 155 • 156

## PETS WELCOME
The owners of these places are happy to discuss the idea of your bringing your pet with you.

### Northern Portugal
Minho
4 • 7 • 10 • 13 • 14 • 15 • 16 • 18 • 19 • 22
Tràs-os-montes
24 • 25 • 26 • 28 • 30
Douro
36 • 37 • 39 • 44

### Central Portugal
Beira
46 • 49 • 50 • 52 • 56 • 58 • 60 • 62 • 63 • 64 •
Estremadura
74 • 75 • 86 • 87 •
Ribatejo
91 • 93 • 96 • 97 • 100 • 101 • 102

### Southern Portugal
Alentejo
103 • 108 • 109 • 112 • 113 • 115 • 116 • 117 • 118 • 120 122 • 125
Algarve
133 • 134 • 141 • 144 • 148 • 155

The Azores
158

## BIKE

You can either borrow or hire bikes at these places.

### Northern Portugal
Minho
5 • 7 • 9 • 15 • 22 • 23

Tràs-os-montes
26 • 27 • 28
Douro
32 • 34 • 38 • 39

### Central Portugal
Beira
46 • 47 • 48 • 51 • 54 • 56 • 61 • 62
Estremadura
69 • 71 • 74 • 86
Ribatejo
90 • 91 • 92 • 94 • 95 • 100

### Southern Portugal
Alentejo
102 • 103 • 108 • 112 • 113 • 115 • 116 • 118 • 120 • 121 124 •130

Algarve
131 • 134 • 135 • 136 • 137 • 138 • 142 • 144 • 147 • 150 151 • 152 • 153 • 154 • 155

## Non-smoking
These places do not allow smoking on the premises.

### Northern Portugal
Minho
20
Douro
37

### Central Portugal
Estremadura
78

### Southern Portugal
Algarve
148 • 149 • 153

# The music of Portugal

Amália Rodrigues

The lights are low and two players are crouched over their instruments, one the pear-shaped *guitarra* with 12 metal strings, the other the gut-strung guitar. They begin playing a plaintive, passionate melody and then a woman steps forward. Her head is thrown back, her eyes are half closed, and she sings of love in the simple, open-throated manner dictated by long tradition. Against the simple rhythm and silvery lines of the *guitarra* she sings as freely as a jazz player, and the push and pull of her melodic improvisation, the ornamental flourishes and emotional intensity, command complete attention from the audience.

This is Portuguese *fado*, and the word, from the Latin *fatum*, means 'fate'. These songs of fate and destiny have come from the backstreets, but *fado*'s origins are older, in Brazil and Africa, in songs brought home by sailors and heard in quayside taverns. The songs, sung by men and women, are about the myriad variations on the themes of love, broken hearts and *saudades*, the yearnings of the soul, and about the old quarters of Lisbon, such as Mouraria, Alfama and Bairro Alto.

Probably the greatest *fado* singer of them all was Amália Rodrigues (1921-1999). She began as a fruit seller in the streets of Lisbon, singing for pleasure, and rose to become an international star and a Portuguese icon. She said: "The *fado* is a song of the soul, a kind of cry. In Portugal, when something sad happens, you say 'It was my *fado*'. It's a music which touches people all over the world. The *fado* is very simple, with almost no harmony or melody. You could say that they're poor songs, and that you have to be rich inside to sing *fado* well. I can't rehearse a *fado* and sing it one way tonight and the same way tomorrow. I don't know how to do that. I sing from the heart, without process or techniques, with nothing but me and my voice." Today you can judge her genius for yourself, for numerous recordings by Amália are available.

# The music of Portugal

The finest fadistas today are probably Cristina Branco, who has a superb and original voice, and Carlos Zel (men also sing *fado*); also worth hearing are Dulce Pontes, Mafalda Arnaud and Mízia, singer of 'new *fado*'.

The *guitarra* players are usually virtuosos who provide counter-melodies to the singers' line and also play instrumentals. One of the greatest was the late Carlos Paredes; others are António Chainho and Luisa Amaro, of the Trio de Guitarras.

One of Portugal's finest and most original groups is undoubtedly Madredeus, featuring the wonderful voice of Teresa Salgueiro; this ensemble, of acoustic guitars, cello and accordion, makes hauntingly beautiful music, truly Portuguese in character, and has achieved international success. Listen to Antologia and O Paraíso. Another original is Rão Kyao (flute and sax); his Fado Bailado is a classic of *fado* melodies.

Although Portugal is considered Latin, many of its roots lie in Celtic culture. The rich and beautiful melodies of the folk music have been beautifully played for years by the Brigada Vitor Jara group. Traditional folk is also the domain of the group *Gaiteiros de Lisboa*. Folk diversity and some of Portugal's finest voices can be heard on the album *Cantigas de Amigos*, by João Balão & José Moz Carrapa.

In the jazz realm, Portugal's finest and most original players include Carlos Martins' *Orquestre Sons da Lusofonia*, António Pinho Vargas (sax & piano), Laurent Philipe (trumpet), the quintets and trios led by Bernardo Moreira (double bass), and the Carlos Barreto Trio.

If you can hear performances by classical pianists Maria Jõao Pires, António Rosado, Pedro Burmester or Artur Pizarro, all of whom have recorded, take the opportunity.

Portugal has many annual music festivals of classical, choral, folk, jazz and rock. Recorded music is good value and the choice is wide, including the delights of Brazil. Happy hunting and listening.

# Portuguese Wine

Legend has it that the Phoenicians brought the vine to Portugal, but it was the Romans who developed viniculture, so well that wine was exported to other parts of the Empire. They were followed by the Swabians, Visigoths and Moors, and despite the Koran's injunctions against *al-cohol* (an Arab word meaning 'the spirit') the Portuguese continued to make wine. Today, most vineyards are owned by farmers with smallholdings who sell their grapes to the local cooperatives. *Vinho tinto* (red), *branco* (white), *verde* (green) and rosé are great value, and when eating out, don't overlook the *vinho da casa* (house wine) - it will probably be excellent; for a few pounds the most discerning palate will be delighted by *a reserva*.

The main wine-producing areas:

### Alentejo

A large, southern area whose wines are among the best. Try the Redondo, Reguengos and Borba reds.

### Algarve

The reds, excellent with food, are light ruby. The dry whites make fine aperitifs.

### Bairrada

A rich, enduring flavour. Look for São João, Aliança, São Domingos, Império and Barroção.

### Colares

On the Atlantic coast the vines flourish between cane windbreaks. The reds are full of aromatic fruit and in time have a velvety taste.

### Dão

Most wine from these hilly terraces is red, with strong colour and a taste with real bite. Try São João, Grão Vasco, Acácio, Rittos and Caves Velhas.

### Douro

This northern valley was originally demarcated only for port, but now over half the grapes are for light wines. Try Barca Velha, Penajora, Champalimaud and Acácio.

### Port wines

Only made in the Douro. When enough sugar has been converted into alcohol, fermentation is stopped by adding the wine to grape brandy in a ratio of 4:1. Maturation varies and port wine ranges from 19-22 degrees for red and 16.5-20 for white.

# Portuguese Wine

### Oeste

This region produces excellent reds including the rather dry, cedary flavours from Óbidos, the softer Alenquer and the gutsy Arruda reds.

### Ribatejo

Here the vine flourishes in poor soil, but also in the rich flood plains of the Tagus. Reds are deep in colour, with a fruity taste and aftertaste. Sample Caves Velhas Romeira, Teobar of Dom Teodósio, Almeiria and Torre Velha.

### Vinho Verde

This means 'green wine', but the colour is pale yellow. The name is given because of the wine's young taste and because the extreme north, where the vines grow, has more rain and greener countryside. Rather than the usual uniform rows, the vines ramble freely over hedges, houses and pergolas. Vinho verdes are light and perfect with seafood. Try Alvarinho, João Pires, Gatão, Lagosta, Solar das Boucas and Palácio de Brejoeira.

*Vinho tinto*

*branco*

*vinho da casa*

*verde*

# A short history of the Company

Perhaps the best clue as to why these books have their own very particular style and 'bent' lies in Alastair's history.

After a law degree, a stint as a teacher in Voluntary Service Overseas led to a change in direction. He became a teacher (French and Spanish) and then a refugee worker, then spent several years in overseas development work before settling into environmental campaigning, and even green politics. Meanwhile, he was able to dabble - just once a year - in an old interest, taking clients on tours of special places all over Europe. This grew, eventually, into a travel company (it still exists as Alastair Sawday's Tours, operating, inter alia, walking and biking tours all over Europe).

Trying to take his clients to eat and sleep in places that were not owned by corporations and assorted bandits he found dozens of very special places in France - farms, châteaux etc - a list that grew into the first book, *French Bed and Breakfast*. It was a celebration of 'real' places to stay and the remarkable people who run them.

So, this publishing company is based on the success of that first and rather whimsical French book. It started as mild crusade, and there it stays. For we still celebrate the unusual, the beautiful, the highly individual. We have no rules for owners; they do things their own way. We are passionate about rejecting the ugly, the cold, the banal and the indifferent and we are still passionate about promoting the use of 'real' food. Alastair is a trustee of the Soil Association and keen to promote organic growing especially.

It is a source of huge pleasure to us that we seem to have pressed the right button: there are thousands and thousands of people who, clearly, share our views and take up our ideas. We are by no means alone in trumpeting the virtues of standing up to the monstrous uniformity of so much of our culture.

The greatest accolade we have had was in *The Bookseller* magazine, which described us as 'head and shoulders above the rest'. That meant a lot. But even more satisfying is that we are building a company in which people matter. We are delighted to hear of new friendships between those in the books and those using them and to know that there are many people - among them artists, farmers, champions of the countryside - who have been enabled to pursue their unusual lives thanks to the extra income the books bring them.

Of course we want the company to flourish, but this isn't just about money; it is about people, too.

## Alastair Sawday
# Special Places to Stay series

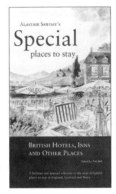

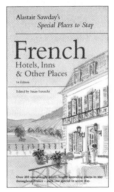

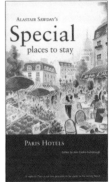

Tel:  **01275 464891**
Fax: **01275 464887**
www.sawdays.co.uk

# The Little Earth Book

The Little Earth Book

Alastair Sawday, the publisher of this (wonderful) guidebook, is also an environmentalist. For over 25 years he has campaigned, not only against the worst excesses of modern tourism and its hotels, but against environmental 'looniness' of other kinds. He has fought for systems and policies that might enable our beautiful planet - simply - to survive. He founded and ran Avon Friends of the Earth, has run for Parliament, and has led numerous local campaigns. He is now a trustee of the Soil Association, experience upon which he draws in this remarkable new book.

Researched and written by an eminent Bristol architect, James Bruges, *The Little Earth Book* is a clarion call to action, a mind-boggling collection of mini-essays on today's most important environmental concerns, from global warming and poisoned food to economic growth, Third World debt, genes and 'superbugs'. Undogmatic but sure-footed, the style is light, explaining complex issues with easy language, illustrations and cartoons. Ideas are developed chapter by chapter, yet each one stands alone. It is an easy browse.

*The Little Earth Book* provides hope, with new ideas and examples of people swimming against the current, of bold ideas that work in practice. It is a book as important as it is original. One has been sent to every M.P. Now you, too, can learn about the issues and join the most important debate of this century.

Oh - one last thing: *The Little Earth Book* is a damned good read! Note what Jonathon Porritt says about it:

**"The Little Earth Book is different. And instructive. And even fun."**

Did you know.....

- If everyone adopted the Western lifestyle we would need five earths to support us

- 60% of infections picked up in hospitals are now drug-resistant

- Environmental disasters have already created 80 MILLION refugees.

# Order Form UK

All these books are available in major bookshops or you may order them direct. Post and packaging are FREE.

| | Price | No. copies |
|---|---|---|
| *Special Places to Stay:* **Portugal** | | |
| Edition 1 | £8.95 | |
| | | |
| *Special Places to Stay:* **Spain** | | |
| Edition 4 | £11.95 | |
| | | |
| *Special Places to Stay:* **Ireland** | | |
| Edition 3 | £10.95 | |
| | | |
| *Special Places to Stay:* **Paris Hotels** | | |
| Edition 3 | £8.95 | |
| | | |
| *Special Places to Stay:* **Garden Bed & Breakfast** | | |
| Edition 1 | £10.95 | |
| | | |
| *Special Places to Stay:* **French Bed & Breakfast** | | |
| Edition 6 | £13.95 | |
| | | |
| *Special Places to Stay:* **British Hotels, Inns** and other places | | |
| Edition 2 | £10.95 | |
| | | |
| *Special Places to Stay:* **British Bed & Breakfast** | | |
| Edition 5 | £12.95 | |
| | | |
| *Special Places to Stay:* **French Hotels, Inns** and other places | | |
| Edition 1 | £11.95 | |
| | | |
| *Special Places to Stay:* **Italy** (from Rome to the Alps) | | |
| Edition 1 | £9.95 | |
| | | |
| **The Little Earth Book** | £4.99 | |

Please make cheques payable to: **Alastair Sawday Publishing**    **Total**

Please send cheques to: Alastair Sawday Publishing, The Home Farm Stables, Barrow Gurney, Bristol BS48 3RW. **For credit card orders call 01275 464891 or order directly from our website www.sawdays.co.uk**

Name:

Address:

Postcode:

Tel:            Fax:

If you do not wish to receive mail from other companies, please tick the box ❑          Po1

# Order Form USA

All these books are available at your local bookstore, or you may order direct. Allow two to three weeks for delivery.

| | Price | No. copies |
|---|---|---|
| ***Special Places to Stay:* Ireland**<br>Edition 3 | $17.95 | |
| ***Special Places to Stay:* Spain**<br>Edition 1 | $17.95 | |
| ***Special Places to Stay:* Paris Hotels**<br>Edition 3 | $14.95 | |
| ***Special Places to Stay:* French Hotels, Inns** and other places<br>Edition 1 | $19.95 | |
| ***Special Places to Stay:* French Bed & Breakfast**<br>Edition 6 | $19.95 | |
| ***Special Places to Stay:* Garden Bed & Breakfast**<br>Edition 1 | $17.95 | |
| ***Special Places to Stay:* British Bed & Breakfast**<br>Edition 5 | $19.95 | |
| ***Special Places to Stay:* British Hotels, Inns and other places**<br>Edition 2 | $17.95 | |
| ***Special Places to Stay:* Italy (from Rome to the Alps)**<br>Edition 1 | $14.95 | |

Shipping in the continental USA: $3.95 for one book,
$4.95 for two books, $5.95 for three or more books.
Outside continental USA, call (800) 243-0495 for prices.
For delivery to AK, CA, CO, CT, FL, GA, IL, IN, KS, MI, MN, MO, NE,
NM, NC, OK, SC, TN, TX, VA, and WA, please add appropriate sales tax

**Please make checks payable to: The Globe Pequot Press**   Total

To order by phone with MasterCard or Visa: (800) 243-0495. 9 a.m. to 5 p.m.
EST; by fax: (800) 820-2329, 24 hours; through our Website: www.globe-pequot.com; or by mail: The Globe Pequot Press, P.O. Box 480, Guilford,
CT 06437.

Name:                          Date:

Address:

Town:

State:                         Zip code:

Tel:                           Fax:

Po1

# Report Form

**Comments on existing entries and new discoveries.**

If you have any comments on entries in this guide, please let us have them.
If you have a favourite house, hotel, inn or other new discovery, please let
us know about it.

Report on:

Entry no: _____ Edition: _____

New recommendation: _____

Name of property: _____

Address: _____

_____

_____ Postcode: _____

Tel: _____

Comments: _____

_____

_____

_____

_____

_____

_____

_____

From: _____

Address: _____

_____

_____ Postcode: _____

Tel: _____

Please send the completed form to: **Alastair Sawday Publishing,
The Home Farm Stables, Barrow Gurney, Bristol BS48 3RW**

Thank you.

# Reservation form

*Á Atençèo de:*
To:

Date:

Estimado Senhor/Estimada Senhora,

*Agradeciamos que efectuassem uma reserva em nome de:*
Please could you make us a reservation in the name of:

| *Para* | *noite(s)* | *Chegada a: dia* | *mês* | *ano* |
|--------|-----------|------------------|-------|-------|
| For | night(s) | Arriving:day | month | year |
| | | *Partida a: dia* | *mês* | *ano* |
| | | Leaving: day | month | year |

| *Desejamos* | *quarto,* | *:* |
|-------------|-----------|-----|
| We would like | rooms, arranged as follows: | |

| *Duplo* | *Camos seperadas* |
|---------|-------------------|
| Double bed | Twin beds |
| *Triplo* | *Individual* |
| Triple | Single |
| *Suite* | *Apartamento* |
| Suite | Appartment |

| *Também desejamos jantar:* | *Sim* | *Não* | *Para* | *pessoas* |
|----------------------------|-------|-------|--------|-----------|
| We will also be requiring dinner | yes | no | for | person(s) |

*Agradeciamos que nos enviassem confirmação desta reserva para o endereço
acima mencionado. (Pode utilizar este formulário ou uma fotocópia do mesmo
com a sua assinatura.)*
Please could you send us confirmation of our reservation to the address
below (this form or a photocopy of it with your signature could be used).

*Nome:* **Name:**

*Endereço:* **Address:**

Tel No:                    E-mail:

Fax No:

**Formulário de Reserva - Special Places to Stay: Portugal**

# Index by house name

# Index by house name

# Index by place name

# Index by place name

# Exchange rate table

| Esc | Euro | US $ | £ Sterling |
|---|---|---|---|
| 50 | 0.25 | 0.24 | 0.16 |
| 100 | 0.50 | 0.48 | 0.32 |
| 500 | 2.50 | 2.40 | 1.60 |
| 1000 | 5.00 | 4.80 | 3.20 |
| 1200 | 6.00 | 5.76 | 3.84 |
| 1500 | 7.50 | 7.20 | 4.80 |
| 2000 | 10.00 | 9.60 | 6.40 |
| 5000 | 25.00 | 24.00 | 16.00 |
| 10000 | 50.00 | 48.00 | 32.00 |
| 15000 | 75.00 | 72.00 | 48.00 |
| 20000 | 100.00 | 96.00 | 64.00 |
| 25000 | 125.00 | 120.00 | 80.00 |
| 30000 | 150.00 | 144.00 | 96.00 |
| 40000 | 200.00 | 192.00 | 128.00 |
| 50000 | 250.00 | 240.00 | 160.00 |

Rates correct at time of going to press January 2001

## Spoofs

All our books have the odd spoof hidden away within their pages. Sunken boats, telephone boxes and ruined castles have all featured. Some of you have written in with your own ideas. So, we have decided to hold a competition for spoof writing every year.

The rules are simple: send us your own spoofs, include the photos, and let us know which book it is intended for. We will publish the winning entries in the following edition of each book. We will also send a complete set of our guides to each winner.

Please send your entries to:

**Alastair Sawday Publishing, Spoofs competition,**
**The Home Farm Stables, Barrow Gurney,**
**Bristol BS48 3RW.**
**Winners will be notified by post.**

# Symbols

Treat each one as a guide rather than a statement of fact and check important points when booking:

 Working farm.

 Children are positively welcomed, with no age restrictions, but cots, high chairs etc are not necessarily available.

 Pets are welcome but may have to sleep in an outbuilding or your car. Check when booking.

 Vegetarians catered for with advance warning.

 Owners use only certified organic produce.

 Most, but not necessarily all, ingredients are organic, organically grown, home-grown or locally grown.

 Full and approved wheelchair facilities for at least one bedroom and bathroom and access to all ground-floor common areas.

 Basic ground-floor access for people of limited mobility and at least one bedroom and bathroom accessible without steps, but not full facilities for wheelchair-bound guests.

 No smoking anywhere in the house.

 Smoking restrictions exist, usually, but not always in the dining room and some bedrooms. For full restrictions, check when booking.

 This house has pets of its own that live in the house: dog, cat, duck, parrot...

 Credit cards accepted; most commonly Visa and MasterCard.

 Your hosts speak English, whether perfectly or not.

 You can either borrow or hire bikes here.

 Payment by cash or cheques only.

 Swimming pool on the premises.

 Air conditioning in bedrooms. It may be a centrally operated system or individual apparatus.

157   Entry numbers in green means premises are uninspected.